KATSUSHIKA HOKUSAI

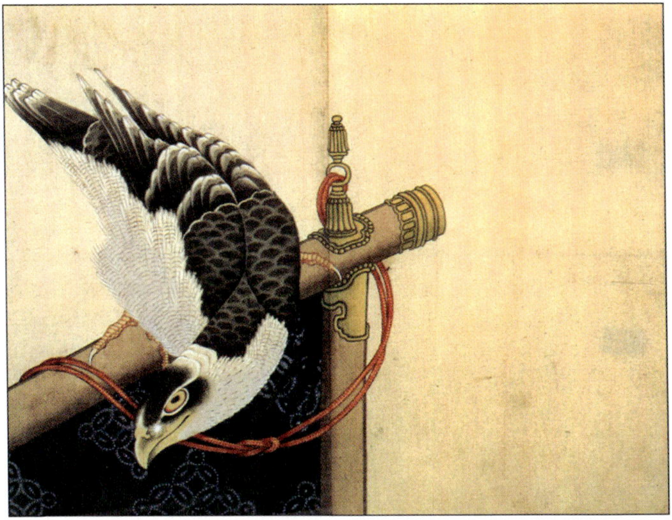

T&J

Published by TAJ Books International LLC 2013
219 Great Lake Drive
Cary, North Carolina, USA
27519

www.tajbooks.com
www.tajminibooks.com

All notations of errors or omissions (author inquiries, permissions) concerning the content of this book should be addressed to

info@tajbooks.com.

ISBN 978-1-84406-262-1

Printed in China.

1 2 3 4 5 17 16 15 14 13

KATSUSHIKA HOKUSAI

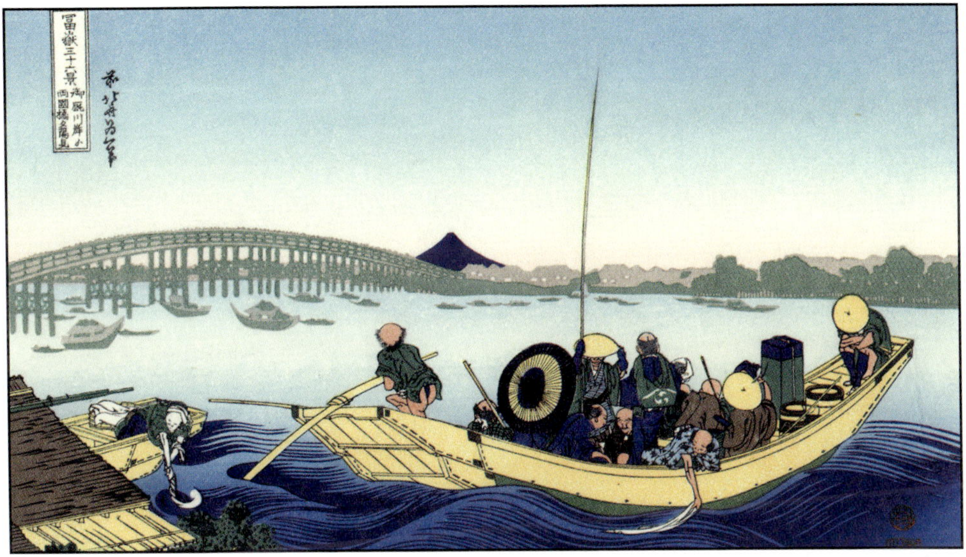

T&J

BY SANDRA FORTY

KATSUSHIKA HOKUSAI

1760–1849

Katsushika Hokusai is the most famous of a sequence of names used by a versatile and long-lived Japanese artist who worked in many genres and schools, absorbing techniques from both inside and outside his own culture. In this way, he evolved a unique style and became a true master, creating new forms in the various media in which he worked. Hokusai's name changes mirrored spiritual, artistic, and physical developments in his own life. He was an unusual and restless man who slipped boundaries and made fresh connections, yet never sought great wealth or position, staying true to himself and to his art.

Even for such a long career his output was staggering. He produced over 30,000 different designs, prints, illustrations, paintings, and sketches. Hokusai is particularly known for transforming the traditional one-dimensional landscape color woodblock print with perspective. This evolution made him seem radical and almost foreign to his countrymen, because conventional Japanese appreciation was more traditional and restrained. His impact was felt far beyond Japan, influencing many other artists, including the French Impressionists. His long career spanned the golden age of the Tokugawa Shogunate, before Japan opened up to the outside world, but at the point that the feudal military society was beginning to change. The Shogunate's success ensured peace during which wealth and literacy prospered, allowing the development of a strong middle class, centered in Edo, the eastern capital of the de facto ruler of Japan, the Shogun.

With income to spend, yet no land or power, the middle class created a safety-valve fantasy world of beauty and pleasure called the Floating World situated in Yoshiwara, Edo's licensed red-light district. Filled with teahouses, brothels, and Kabuki theaters, life's fleeting pleasures and poignancy as well as the beauty of nature were celebrated along with more earthly desires. The development of *ukiyo-e* (floating-world pictures) woodblock prints was one aspect of this culture. The prints depicted *geisha*, *baijin* (beautiful women), courtesans, famous Kabuki actors, and Sumo wrestlers along with myths, ghost stories, and tales of legendary Samurai.

Hokusai is famous for covering the whole spectrum of ukiyo-e art: individual and series prints, *surimono* (fine long-format greeting cards), picture books, books of anecdotes, illustrations of verse and historical romances, erotic books, paintings, and sketches. Regardless of the medium or format, Hokusai seems to capture the essence of what he sees in a way that transcends time and makes it seem continually contemporary—and therein lies his genius.

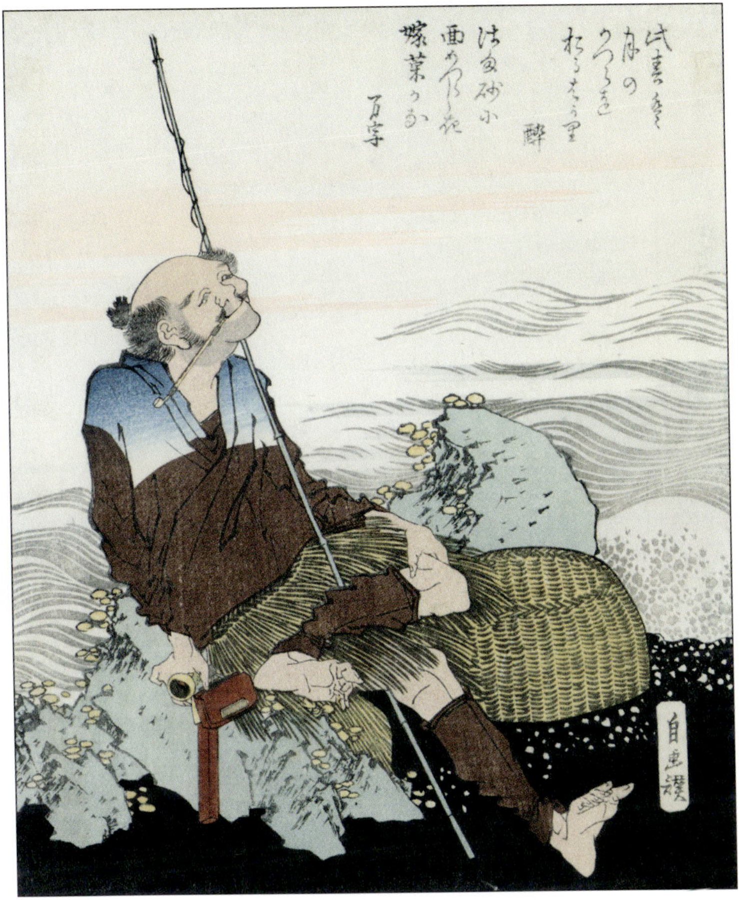

Hokusai's self-portrait, as a fisherman

Hokusai was born in late 1760 in Honjo Warigesui near the Sumida River in Shimoza province, very close to old Edo, now central Tokyo. Not much is known about his original family other than the name Kawamura, one of the names on his gravestone. As the eldest son, he was given the name Tokitaro, which means first-born son. It seems, however, he was not a legitimate heir, and in 1763, he was adopted by a local craftsman, Nakajima Issai, who made illustrated mirrors for the wealthy Samurai elite. The child Tokitaro was renamed Tetsuzo, the first of the many changes of nomenclature that would become a regular feature of his life; Hokusai used over 30 names and claimed to have changed his residence over 90 times. Some names he adopted were other artists' names given in recognition of his work or study by master-run workshop-studios, but most names were his, taken to reflect artistic changes and spiritual motives as well as his different studios and locations around the city and its environs.

At a young age, Hokusai displayed a rather precocious artistic talent and at age 13 or 14 began a brief apprenticeship to a woodblock carver. He also worked for a while in a library/bookshop and developed an interest in sketching life forms and illustration. This grounding in the color engraving and printing processes, as well as other media, marked the beginning of a long journey.

SHUNRO PERIOD, 1779–1794

In 1778, at age 18, Hokusai became an apprentice of Katsukawa Shunsho, who ran the leading studio at the time for the production of *yakusha-e*, or color actor prints. He soon made an impression and was given the name Shunro (spring brightness) in recognition of his work. He produced his first published work within a year. His ukiyo-e prints of Kabuki actors beginning in 1779 show his latent talent, but are really little more than conventional pieces, reflecting his growing dexterity in the school's "house-style" techniques. But this early achievement cannot be diminished. To become a named artist at such a prestigious studio in so short a time is extraordinary, and to outgrow it within a few years, still more so. During the following decade, he would release works under a variety of names: Katsukawa Shunro, Katsu Shunro, Shunro, Kusamura Shunro, Shunro Gunbatei, and Gunbatei.

In 1779, he began publishing works under the name Katsukawa Shunro, making his ukiyo-e debut with the studio's signature actor prints. But he soon showed more variety with *kibyoshi, or* "yellowbacks," which were popular illustrated novels, and *baijinga*, which were prints of beautiful women. His first *hanashi-bon* (humorous stories) prints were created in 1781. Four years later in 1785, he temporarily adopted the name Gunbatei, as he continued to illustrate kibyoshi. He also began to illustrate several humorous books. He was far too independently minded to stay within the tight regime of the studio and as time went by he began to wander artistically.

His next focus was on landscapes and images of the daily life of the Japanese people from many different social levels. One such work was *Fireworks on Ryogoku Bridge*, produced in 1790. Slowly he began to emerge as an artist with a very distinctive style. In 1793, his master, Shunsho, died and he left the Katsukawa school. The circumstances of his leaving are not clear, but perhaps he was expelled by Shunsho's eldest disciple, Shunko, because of his association with the Kano school, which was run by the artist Yusen Hironobu.

Hokusai later said that his leave-taking was a critical confrontation, when he was insulted and belittled by Shunko, and consequently determined to go his own way. He was obviously unconventional and refused to be bound by the narrow confines of a single school. His inquisitive nature extended to all forms of art, from all sources. He continued to study both Japanese and Chinese painting and was also exposed to Western art through French and Dutch engravings he had acquired. By 1794 he was using the new artist's name of Tawaraya Sori.

SORI PERIOD, 1795–1804

When he was 36 years old, Hokusai's work in various styles and types of projects–paintings, surimono, and illustrations–began to fuse into a very unique style. His transition began by joining the Tawaraya Painting Studio, thus entering a stunning creative period. He produced a large number of superb individual prints, illustrations for books as well as some exquisite surimono, a medium he came to excel in. With these works, he began to shift away from the Katsukawa school of actors and courtesans into genre scenes.

Always experimenting, Hokusai continued to study several Japanese painting styles: from the Kano masters he learned the art of brush painting and from the Korin and Tosa schools he derived his wonderful sense of decorative pattern design. He also studied Chinese painting, especially the bird and flower combinations of the Ching and Ming periods. He delved into Western painting under Shiba Kokan, the great pioneer of this approach in Japan at the time. He experimented in the Western manner–using *chiaroscuro* and perspective. His pictures of courtesans and baijin were in a style popularly known as "Sori Beauties." As Hokusai came to dominate the field, he enjoyed many lavish limited-edition commissions, which gave him the opportunity to work at the top end of that market in terms of materials. In this way he became the most successful artist at the Tawaraya School.

Nevertheless, Hokusai, believing that he had reached the end of another creative phase, bestowed his name Sori on the apprentice Soji in 1798 and left the Tawaraya Studio. He adopted a new name, a name that he would use in different combinations until his death: Hokusai. Hokusai was a member of the Nichiren sect of Buddhism. One theory of why he adopted the name is that Polaris, the North Star, is called Hokkyokusei in Japanese and represents the god Myokken, venerated by both Nichiren Buddhists and Shinto followers. Myokken was very popular in Edo. There were many fires in the city, and Myokken protected from fire, brought luck and prosperity, and healed illness of the eyes. He also monitored the behavior of human beings, recording good and bad deeds in a notebook, and was venerated as a special protector deity of the land and country of Japan, holding the secret of immortality.

Another theory about the derivation of the name Hokusai is that it is an abbreviation of Hokushinsai, meaning "North Star Studio." Hokusai was obviously a religious or spiritual man, frugal and cautious, yet warm and spontaneous, who observed life minutely. His changing names reflected the stages of his life—where he lived, what influenced him. And his mystical nature thus supplied the name Hokusai, by which he would be known most widely.

In the early 1800s, Hokusai, using the name Hokusai Tokimasa, was producing humorous *kyoka-bon e-hon* greeting cards and also illustrated books, such as the *1,800 Famous Views of the Eastern Capital*. He then began an extended period of travel into the provinces that would later feature in his works, such as *A Tour of the Waterfalls of the Provinces* and *Unusual Views of Celebrated Bridges in the Provinces*. By 1804, Hokusai seems to have dropped Tokimasa from his name. No doubt it was a change reflecting his further development as a person as well as an artist, or perhaps an overlap in the evolutionary process.

KATSUSHIKA HOKUSAI PERIOD, 1805–1810

Hokusai had announced a burgeoning new style with the name Hokusai Tokimasa, and now he changed his name to Katsushika Hokusai, as he pioneered the world of *yomi-hon* book illustrations. Yomi-hon, or reading books, had fewer illustrations than other book styles of the period. After a series of brush paintings of baijin women, his ukiyo-e began to diverge from portraiture, and he published two collections of landscapes, *Famous Sights of the Eastern Capital* and *Eight Views of Edo*. He also began to attract students of his own—he would have over 50 in the course of his life—as his reputation grew.

His reputation was further enhanced by certain flamboyant live improvisations that he is said to have performed. In 1804 during a temple festival, he painted a massive 600-foot-long picture of Daruma, the Japanese Bhuddist monk, using a broom as a giant brush, with buckets to hold the ink. Another story of his exploits has him winning a competition judged by the Shogun, no less, improvising red maple leaves in the Tatsuta River by painting a single blue line and then letting loose a cock whose feet had been dipped in red ink to traipse across the painting. Initially, these stories seem apocryphal, yet given his skill and his spontaneity, they are not at odds with his more self-effacing underlying character.

In 1805 Hokusai began a series of collaborations, illustrating books with text supplied by the famous writer Takizawa Bakin. The following year, he lived with Bakin for a while and traveled through Kasuza Province. In 1807, he illustrated *Strange Tales of the Crescent Moon*. By the fourth series of collaborations, their stormy relationship and artistic differences led to the project's cancellation. It is a measure of Hokusai's growing esteem that he was kept on by the publisher to work on other projects with other writers, and the next year, he supplied illustrations to a different author. His work at the end of the decade is signed Gakyojin Hokusai, which means "on travels far from home."

TAITO PERIOD, 1810–1820

In this decade, Hokusai continued to produce yomi-hon, but his main focus was on *edehon*—a guide for apprentices that became a universally popular design and sketch collection. In 1810, he published *shunga*, or erotic prints, such as the 12-part sequence *Fukujuso* ("The Adonis Plant"). In this period, he first used the name Taito on his works, followed in 1811 by a brush painting that he signed as Katsushika Hokusai Taito.

In 1812, Hokusai spent the autumn in Nagoya preparing his sketches for publication as *Part One of Hokusai Manga. Manga* are rapid sketches and spontaneous drawings. This classic series would eventually reach 15 volumes of woodcut prints of his sketches; 3 volumes were published posthumously due to overwhelming demand. Over 4,000 drawings make it a truly extraordinary encyclopedia of Japanese life in the Edo Period. Each individual item—animate or inanimate—is observed and recorded with Hokusai's keen eye, fine line, wonderful balance of symmetry and asymmetry, and an obvious delight in the variety of life and nature.

Along with the drawings came suggestions of his art philosophy: "There is a saying of the ancients: Who cannot stand cannot walk, who cannot walk cannot run. To stand is 'shin' (also to copy faithfully), to walk is 'gyo' (also to picture), to run is 'so' (also to dash off a rapid sketch)." Another sentiment found in his work is: "Nothing in Nature is left unattempted." Hokusai's manga were phenomenally popular at the time and are still used by students of drawing today. In 1819, Hokusai moved on yet again, bestowing the name Taito upon an apprentice.

ITSU PERIOD, 1820–1833

To celebrate his milestone 60th birthday in 1820, he adopted a new name: Itsu. Continuing to focus on edehon and manga, his drive and discipline also created time for him to complete some surimono masterworks. This marked the start of a period in which he secured fame as an artist throughout Japan and reached the peak of his career, producing some of his finest and most famous works, including his tour de force, *Thirty-Six Views of Mount Fuji,* in 1831. Among the other popular series of prints he published during this time are *A Tour of the Waterfalls of the Provinces* and *Unusual Views of Celebrated Bridges in the Provinces.*

Hokusai also began producing a number of *kacho-e,* or detailed individual images of flowers and birds, including the extraordinarily detailed *Poppies* and *Flock of Chickens.* Mount Fuji represented a particular fascination for Hokusai because the majestic peak was linked to his religious beliefs; it held a unique mystical significance. Psychologically dominating the country, for centuries Mount Fuji had been accepted as an embodiment of the guardian spirit of Japan. It was traditionally linked with eternal life and can be traced to "The Tale of the Bamboo Cutter," where a goddess deposits the elixir of life on its apex. This secret of immortality was at the heart of Hokusai's own personal obsession with the mountain.

In 1823, he used the name Manji, yet in 1824 produced more edehon under the name Hokusai Itsu. Perhaps he reverted to his earlier name because the previous edehon had been produced under that name or perhaps it was a function of the vagaries of a complicated print production and publishing process.

In 1828, when Hokusai was in his 69th year, his second wife, Kotome, died. He never remarried. His first wife had died in 1793, leaving him alone with a son and two daughters. In 1797 he remarried. Shortly after his second wife's death, Hokusai's daughter and pupil, Oei, an artist in her own right, returned to her father's side, remaining with him the rest of his life. Hokusai's eldest son by his first wife had died in 1812, and one of his daughters had died in 1821. Both of his daughters had unhappy marriages and, after divorcing, both returned to their father's household. Hokusai adopted his eldest daughter's son, but nothing further is really known about his grandson.

The 1830s was a prolific period for the old master. His work featured famous landmarks and symbolic landscapes, exquisitely stylized and rendered, and peopled with all forms of human life in their foregrounds. As well as these stunning landscapes, he produced bird, animal, and insect paintings, flora and fauna prints, surimono, shunga, and illustrations of ghostly tales, famous poets, and literary figures.

During the years 1829 to 1833, Hokusai produced *Fugaku Sanjurokkei–36 Views of Mount Fuji* and *10 Ura Fuji,* 10 views of Mount Fuji from the other side. These paintings are his seminal work by which he is best known. In fact there were eventually 46 individual works in the set. Hokusai added 10 more views after the fact because of the popularity of the series as well as due to his own motivation and obsession with the mountain, a particular inspiration, especially toward the end of his life. No other series comes near the perfection of this design and color–except perhaps Hiroshige's

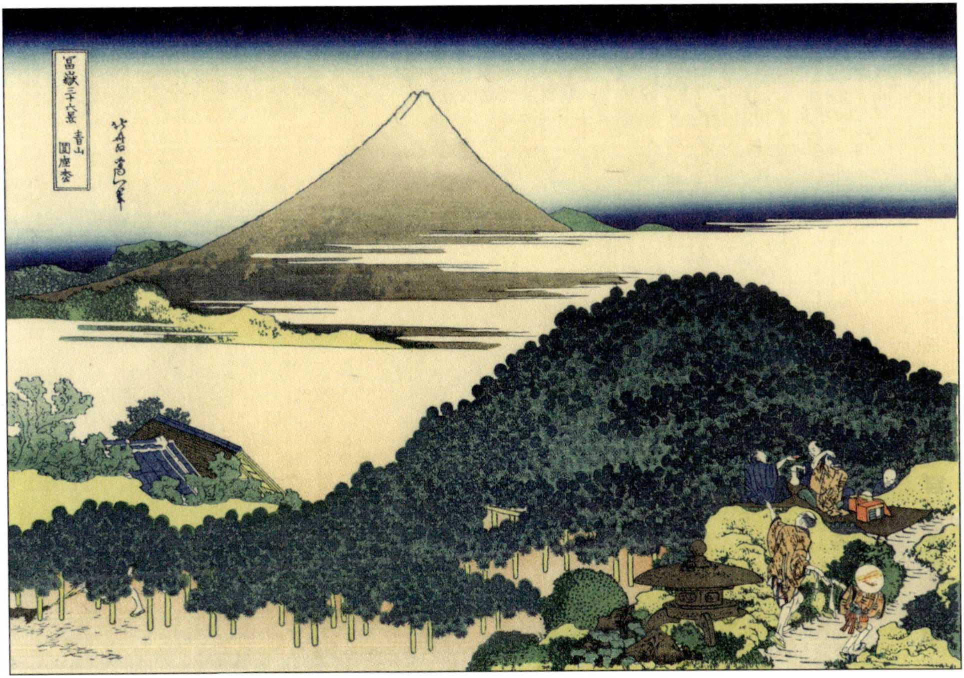

The Circular Pine Trees of Aoyama
from Thirty-Six Views of Mount Fuji, c. 1831–33

53 Stations on the Tokaido. A striking new style synthesized from all the influences and qualities of Hokusai's previous work, coupled with masterful techniques and European perspective, gradually evolved into a unique vision in which the Western technique is reinterpreted and transformed into a design aesthetic that contrasts the nearest and farthest elements of a picture. The colors, too, are exceptional–Prussian blue for example, first imported in 1820, opened up a completely new intensity of color. The *36 Views* glows with a luminous fine blue, apple-green, and dull rich red that are uniquely his own.

MANJI PERIOD 1834–1849

Hokusai focused more on brush painting in his final years. Turning away from conventional subjects, he began to concentrate on myths and legends, flora and fauna yomi-hon, e-hon, and further edehon manuals disclosing his techniques. In 1834 he released his final classic, the exquisite, achromic *Fugaku Hyakkei–100 Views of Mt. Fuji.* He was 75 years old when the first volume was released in 1834. He signed it with the name Hokusai Itsu Gakyo Rojin Manji. His effort to catch the mountain from every angle, in every context, was in the deepest sense a prayer for the gift of immortality that lay hidden within the heart of the recently active volcano. Signaling this quest, he changed his name for the final time: no longer Iitsu, formerly Hokusai, now Gakyo Rojin Manji, translated as "Old Man Mad About Painting." Manji means the "figure of ten thousand" and is the ancient religious symbol of the swastika, giver of life and fortune.

Hokusai's work is in itself a prayer for more time in which to continue striving to realize his vision and improve his technique. Published in three volumes, *100 Views* was published with the famous declaration:

> From the age of six I had a mania for copying the form of things. From about the age of fifty my pictures were frequently published, yet of all I drew prior to the age of seventy there is truly nothing of great note. At the age of seventy-three I finally apprehended something of the true quality of birds, animals, insects, fish, and of the vital nature of grasses and trees. Therefore, at eighty I shall have made some progress, at ninety I shall have penetrated even further the deeper meaning of things, so that at one hundred I shall reach a divine state in my art, and at one hundred and ten, each dot, each line shall surely possess a life of its own. Those of you that live long enough, bear witness that these words of mine prove not false.

Having spent some time out of Edo traveling and staying with friends and admirers, Hokusai returned to the city during a period of famine and for a time found it very difficult to survive, working cheaply in reduced circumstances on anything he could in order to get by. By 1835, the situation had improved and he produced another oban format print series signed with the name Hokusai Manji, followed in 1836 by more *Designs for Craftsmen.*

In 1839, disaster struck as a fire destroyed Hokusai's studio and virtually everything in it except, perhaps, his brushes. Undaunted, he never stopped painting, producing *Ducks in a Stream* at the age of 87. In 1848 he moved his home for the final time, leaving the Honjo quarter for a house near the monastery of Ensho in the Asuka district. Still striving, always stirred by humility, vitality, and wit, he apparently exclaimed on his deathbed, "If heaven gives me ten more years, or even an extension of even five years, I shall surely become a true artist!"

Hokusai died on May 10, 1849, at the age of 89, and was buried at the Senyoko-ji Temple in the Taito Ward of Tokyo. His humble gravestone is inscribed "Tomb of Gwakyo Rojin Manji, of the family of Kawamura. Hokusai of the Province of Shimosa. Famous artist–honest man." His three-line death poem reads: "Even as a ghost, I shall gaily tread, the summer moors."

Only four years after his death, on July 8, 1852, the U.S. Navy's Commodore Perry and his black-hulled steam-driven frigates entered Uraga Harbor, near Edo, and Japan's long era of isolation was over. The opening of the country paved the way for Hokusai's worldwide fame. In Europe, the Art Nouveau (known as Jugendstil in Germany) movement was especially influenced by Hokusai and by Japanese art in general. Japonism began from Hokusai. In fact prominent European artists of the late 19th century and early 20th century who were adherents of a range of artistic styles were equally, if not more, influenced by Hokusai, including Claude Monet, Pierre-Auguste Renoir, Vincent van Gogh, James McNeil Whistler, Edgar Degas, Paul Gauguin, Gustave Klimt, Franz Marc, August Macke, Mary Cassatt, and Edouard Manet. Hokusai's images, his talent, and his ability to portray his deepest feelings about nature, at essence his soul mate, ensure his continued fame throughout the world as a major artist with time-tested allure.

Today Hokusai's art is exhibited in the Guimet Museum in Paris, which owns over 125 individual works; Tokyo National Museum; MOA Museum of Art in Atami, Japan; Brooklyn Museum in New York City; British Museum in London; and private collections. Eight first-edition woodblock prints that compose the series *A Tour of Waterfalls in the Provinces*, dating from about 1833, is in the collection of the Worcester Art Museum in Worcester, Massachusetts.

CARPS

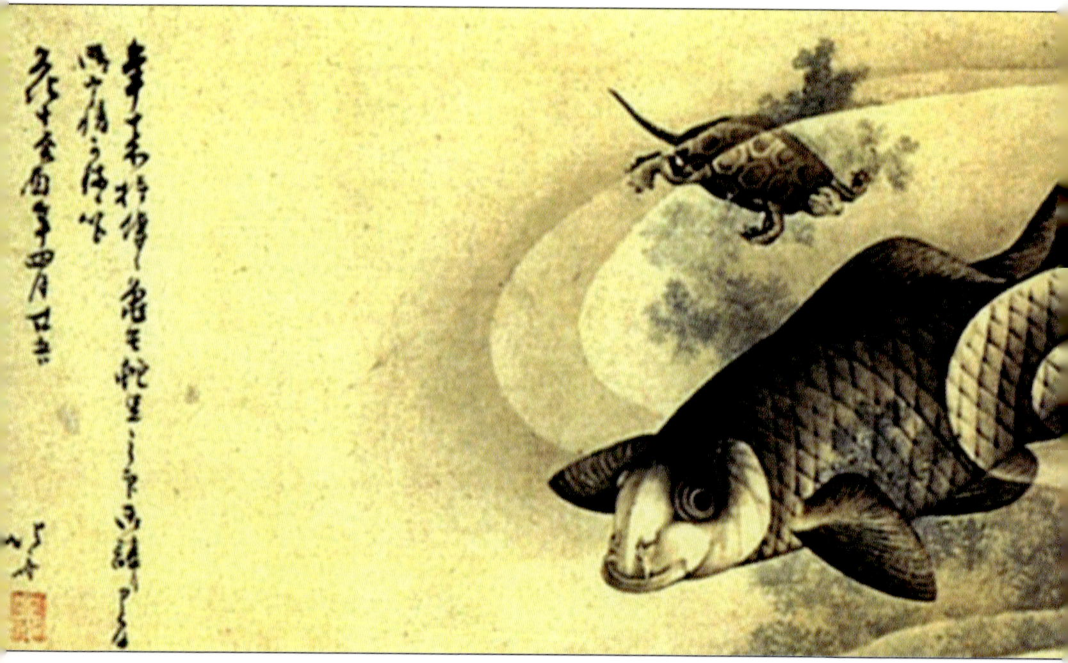

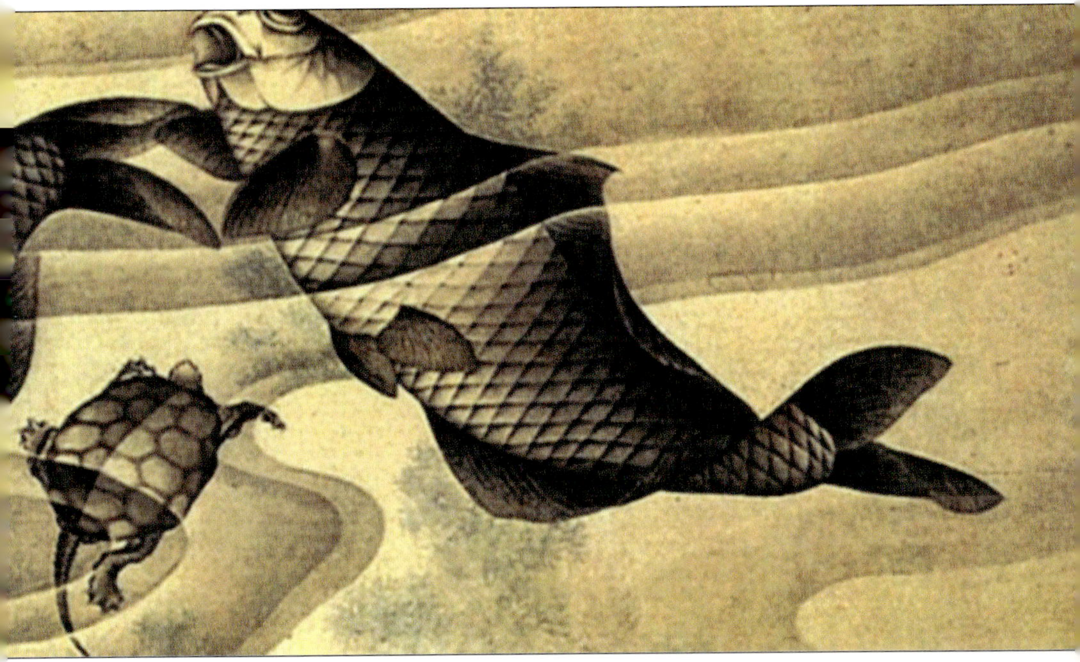

Plate 2

THE WATERFALL OF AMIDA BEHIND THE KISO ROAD

c. 1827, British Museum, London

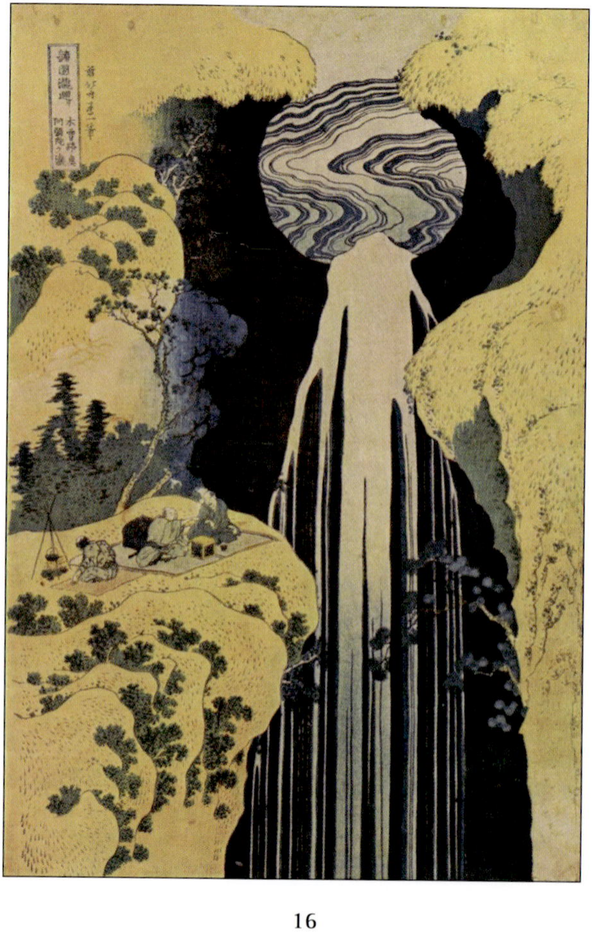

KIRIFURI WATERFALL, MOUNT KUROKAMI, SHIMOTSUKE PROVINCE

c. 1830–31, from A Journey to the Waterfalls of All the Provinces

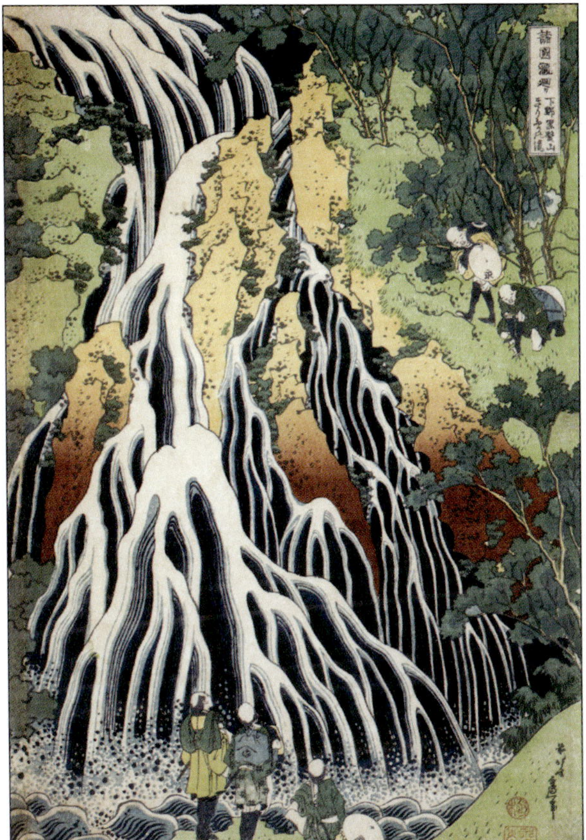

Plate 4

ONO WATERFALL ALONG THE KISOKAIDO

c. 1830–31, from A Journey to the Waterfalls of All the Provinces

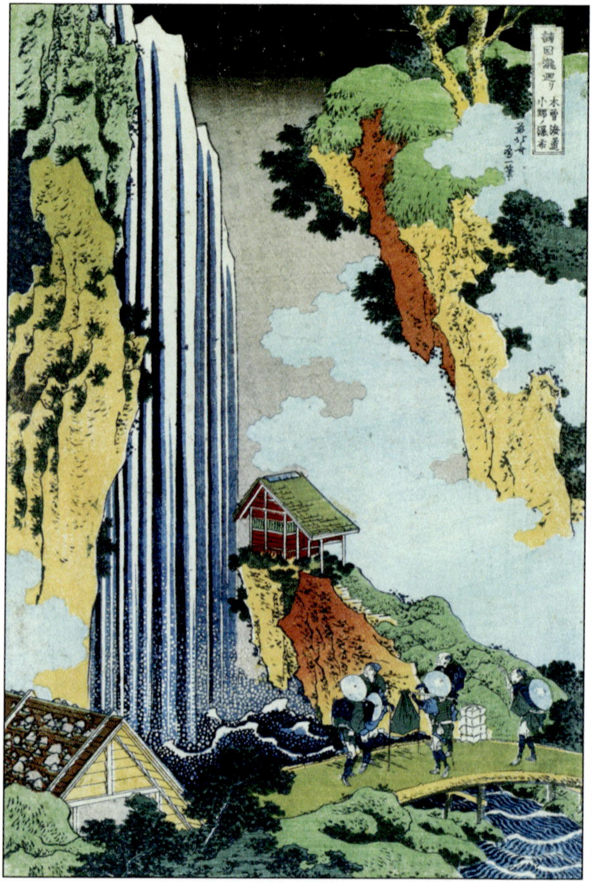

THE AOIGAOKA FALLS IN THE EASTERN CAPITAL

c. 1830–31, from A Journey to the Waterfalls of All the Provinces

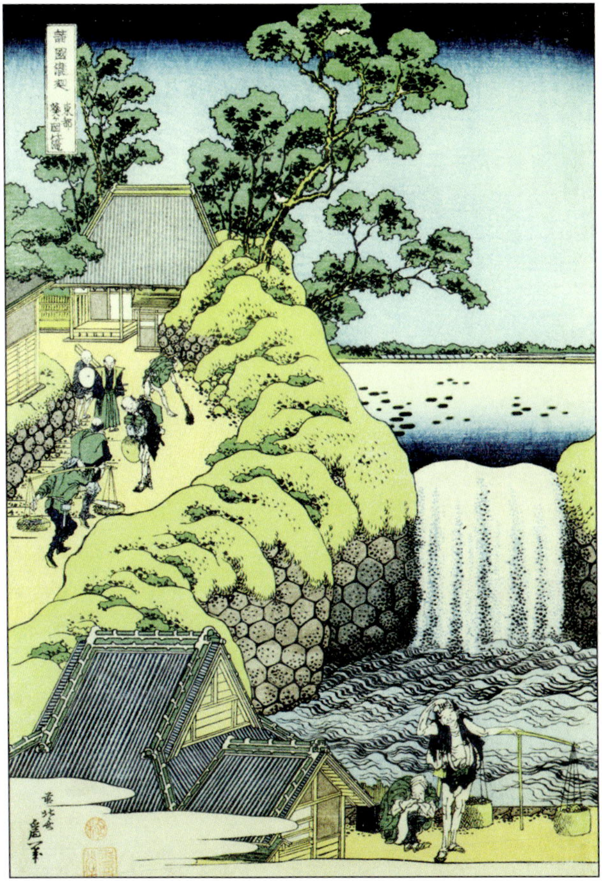

Plate 6

ROBEN WATERFALL OF OYAMA IN SAGAMI PROVINCE

c. 1830–31, from A Journey to the Waterfalls of All the Provinces

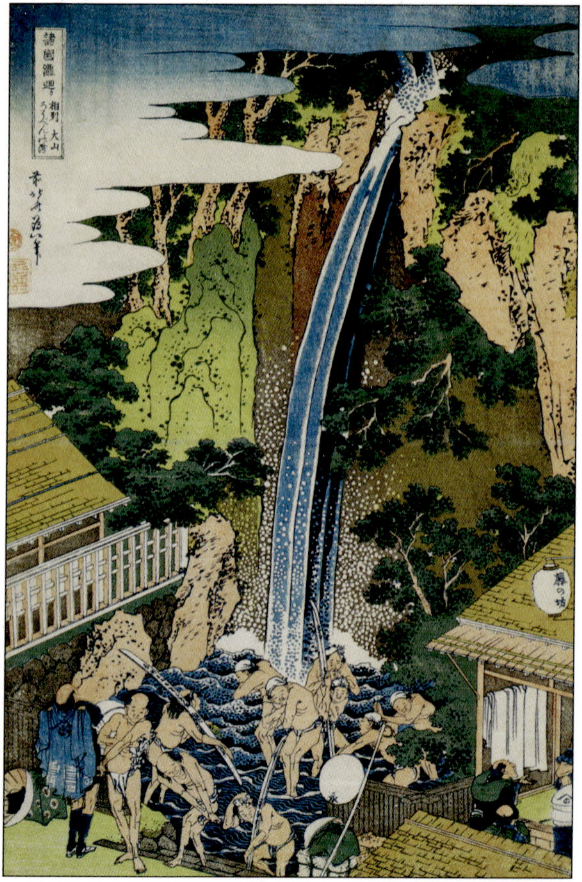

THE YORO FALLS IN MINO PROVINCE

c. 1830–31, from A Journey to the Waterfalls of All the Provinces

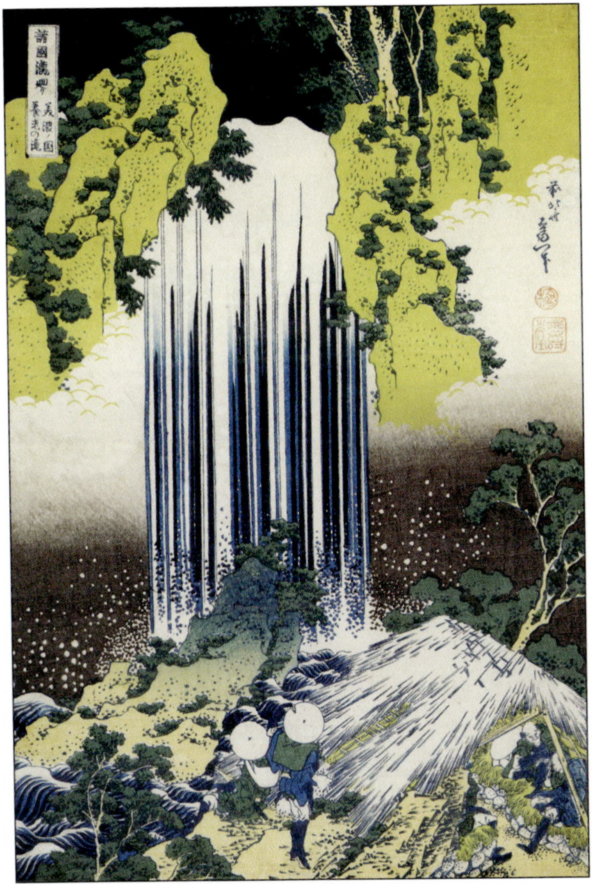

Plate 8

THE WAVE OFF KANAGAWA

1831–33, from Thirty-Six Views of Mount Fuji

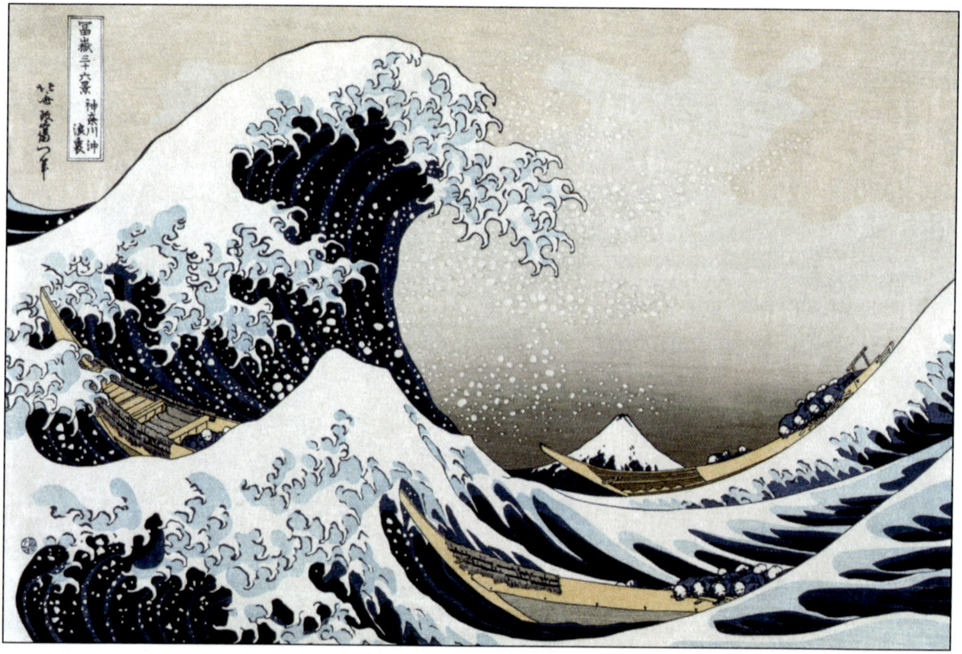

Plate 9

FINE WIND, CLEAR MORNING

1831–33, from Thirty-Six Views of Mount Fuji

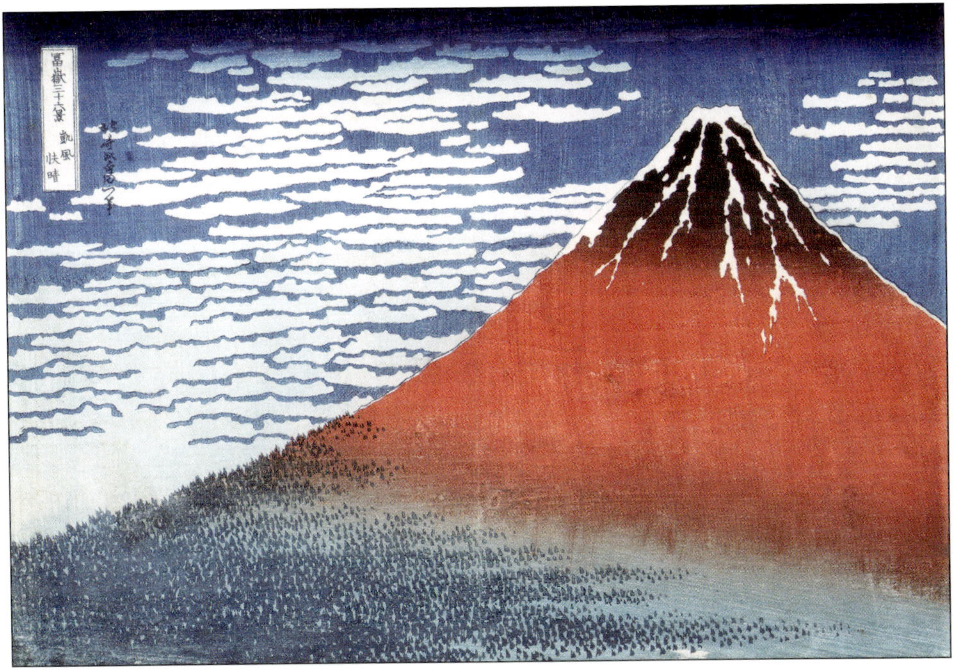

Plate 10

FUJI FROM GOTEN-YAMA, AT SHINAGAWA ON THE TOKAIDO

1831–33, from Thirty-Six Views of Mount Fuji

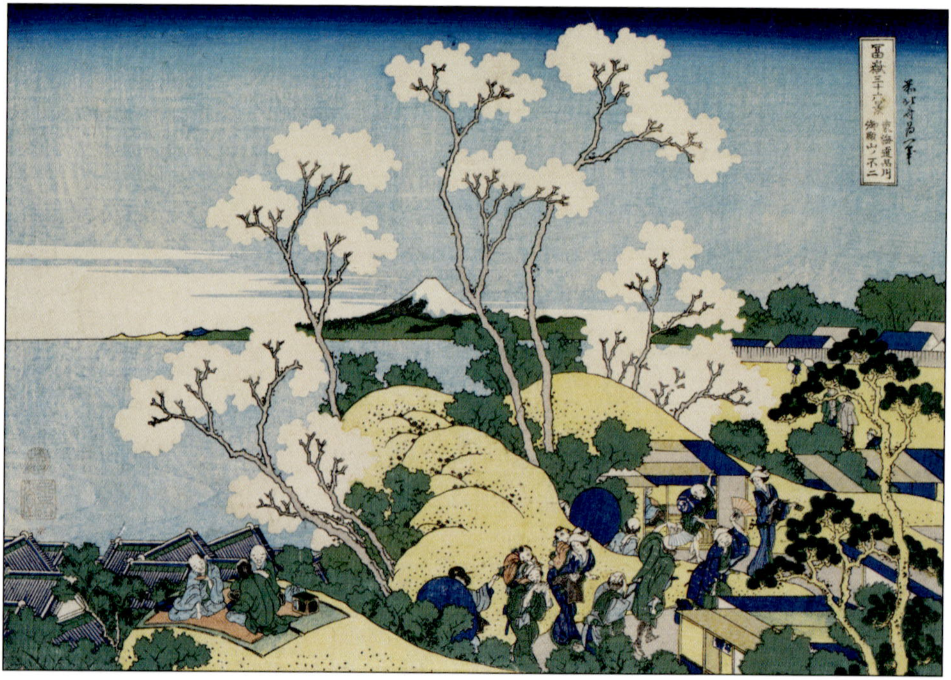

Plate 11

ASAKUSA HONGAN-JI TEMPLE IN THE EASTERN CAPITAL

1831–33, from Thirty-Six Views of Mount Fuji

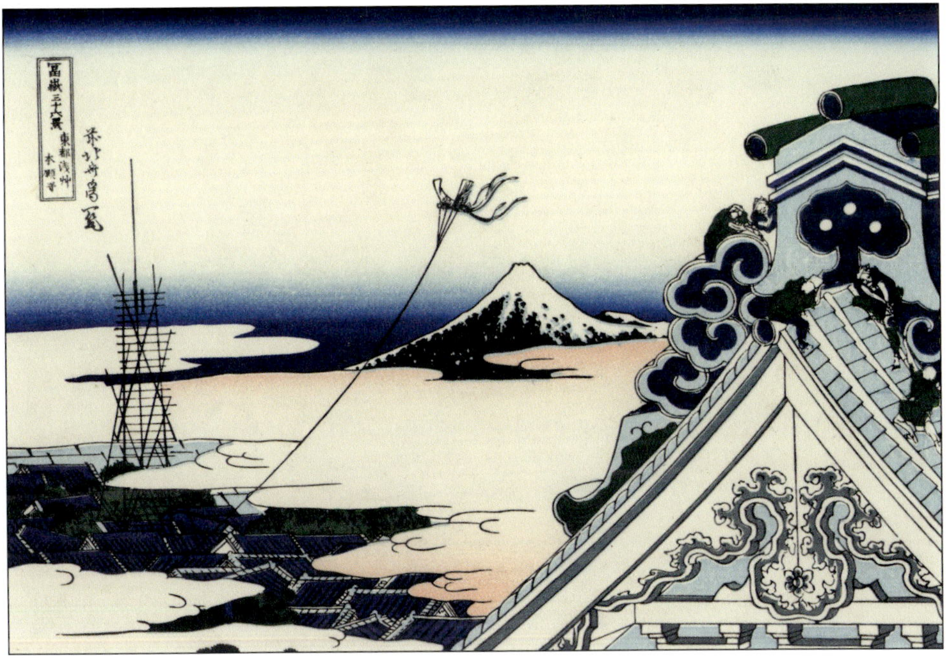

Plate 12

MOUNT FUJI FROM A FIELD IN OWARI PROVINCE

1831–33, from Thirty-Six Views of Mount Fuji

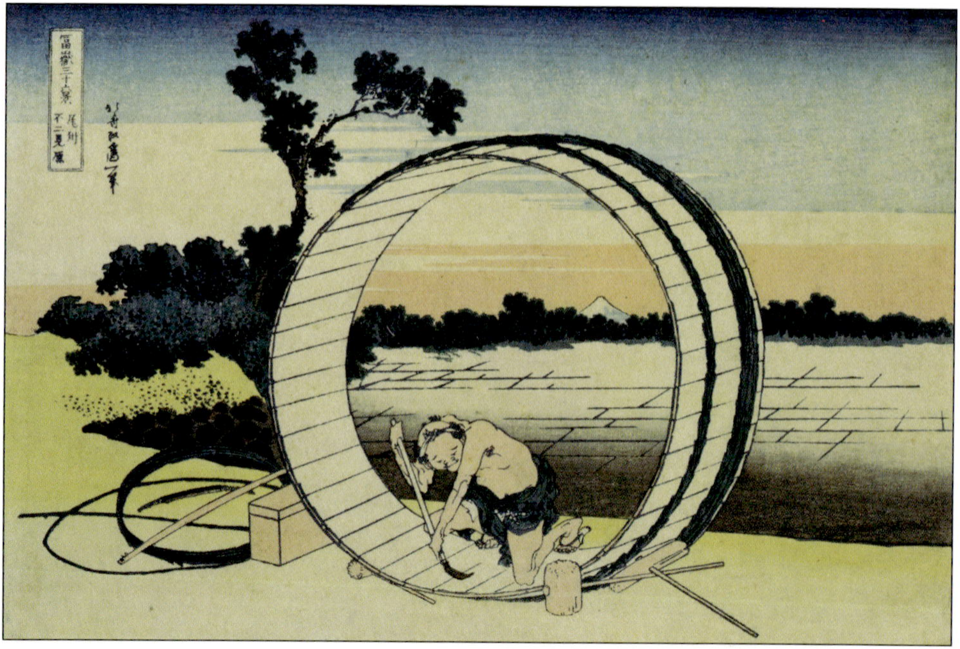

SAZAI HALL OF THE FIVE-HUNDRED-RAKAN TEMPLE

1831–33, from Thirty-Six Views of Mount Fuji

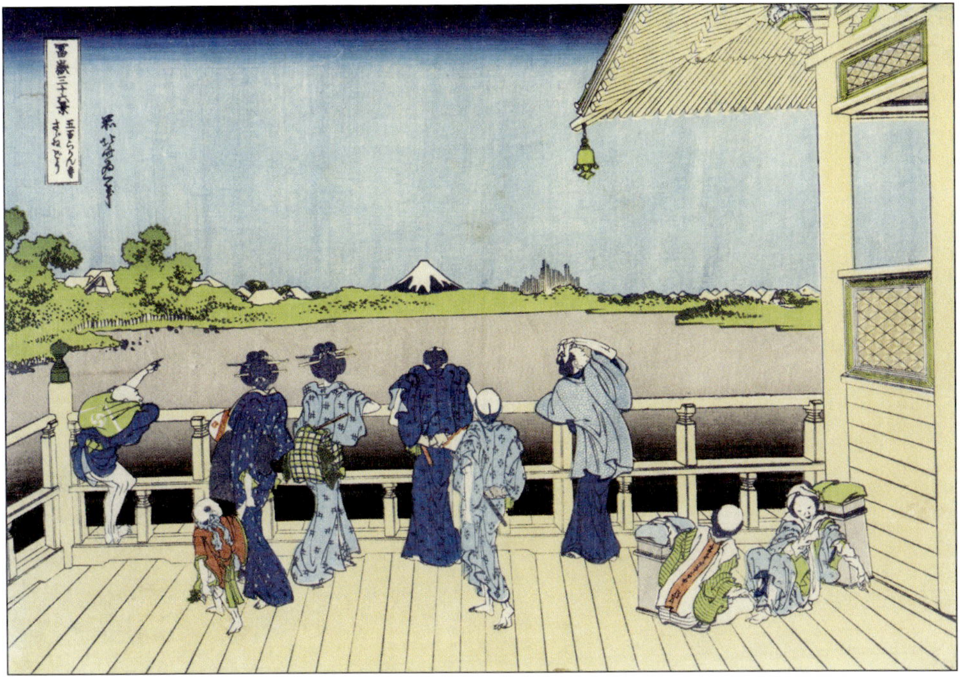

Plate 14

MOUNT FUJI SEEN FROM MISHIMA PASS

1831–33, from Thirty-Six Views of Mount Fuji
Guiment Museum, Paris

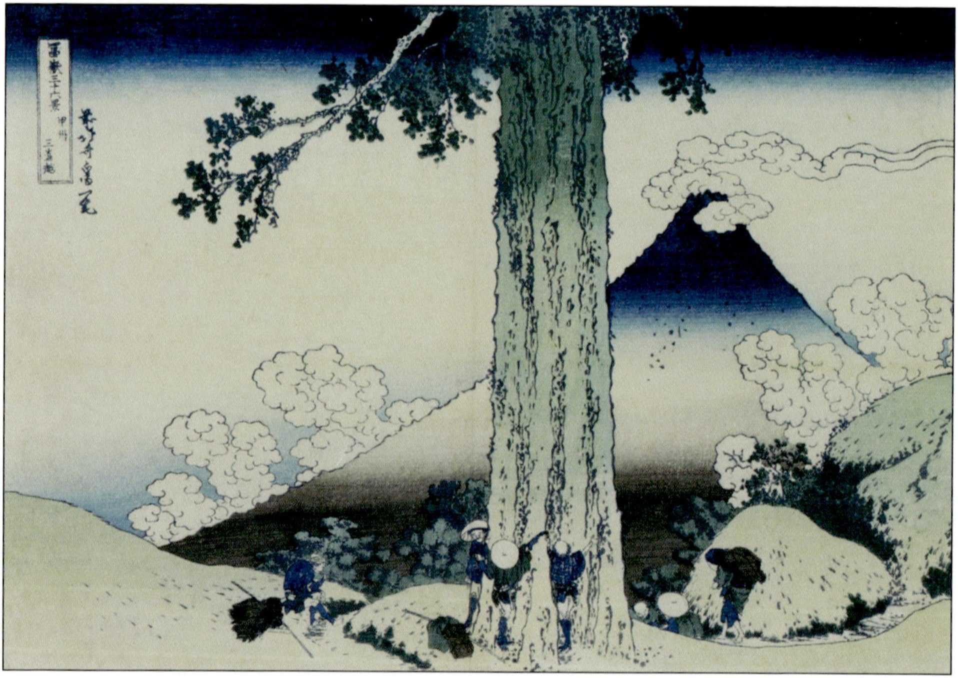

RAINSTORM BENEATH THE SUMMIT

1831–33, from Thirty-Six Views of Mount Fuji

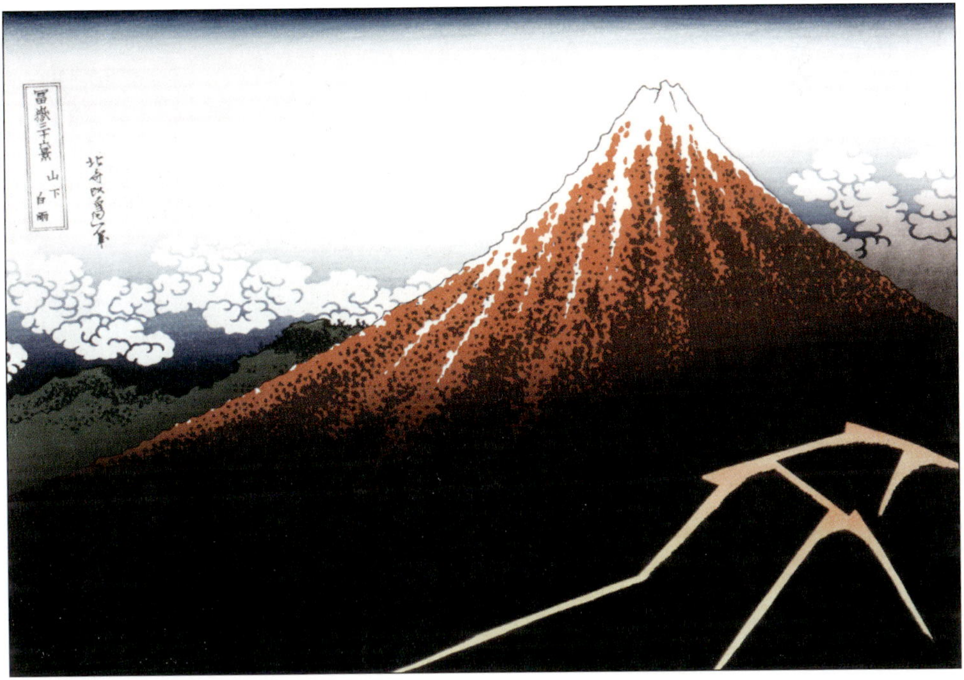

Plate 16

CLIMBING ON MOUNT FUJI

1831–33, from Thirty-Six Views of Mount Fuji

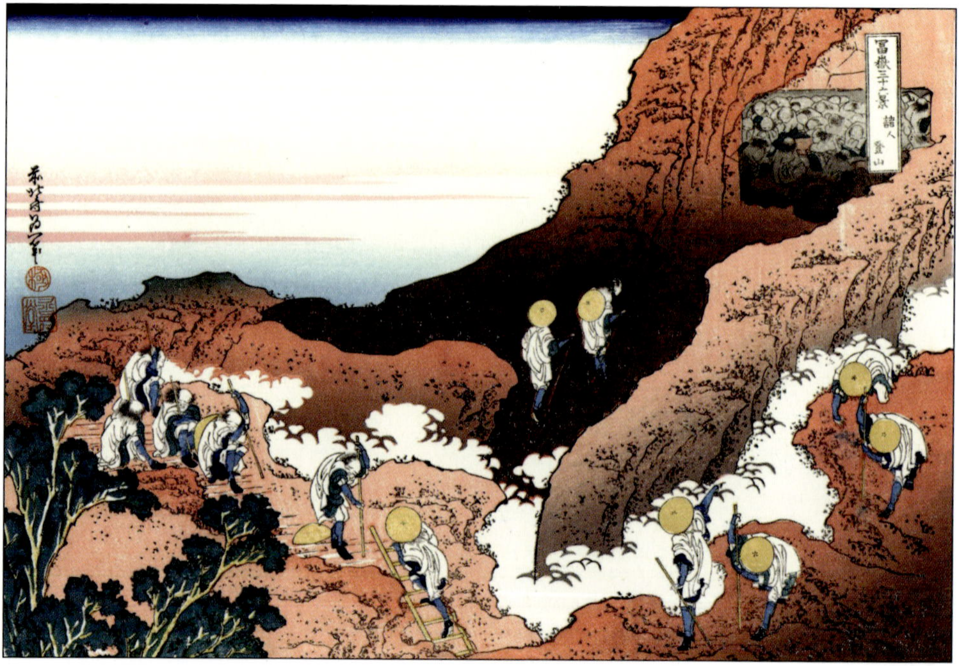

BAY OF NOBOTO

1831–33, from Thirty-Six Views of Mount Fuji

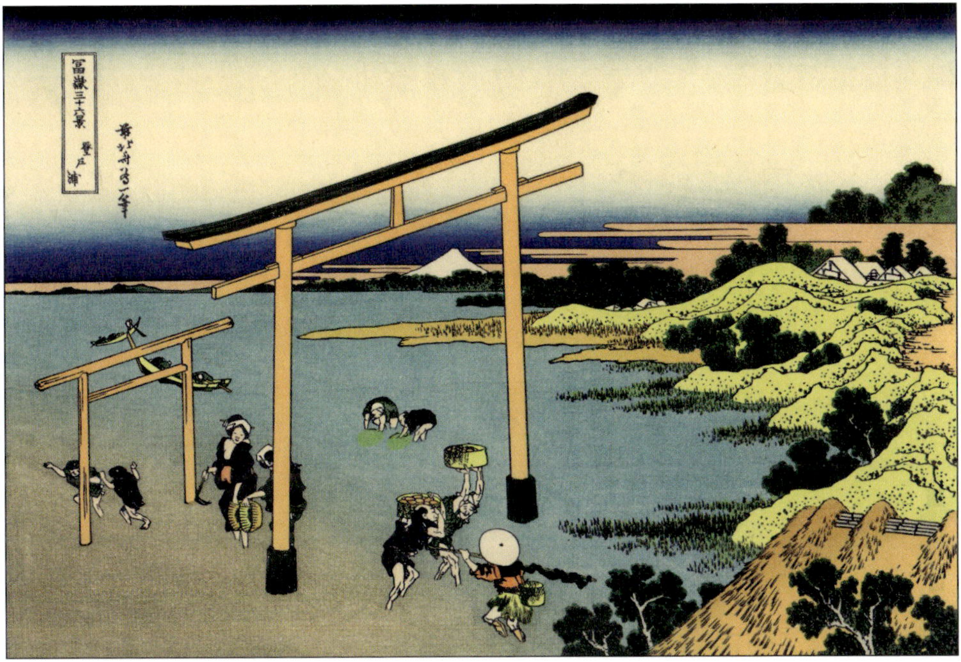

Plate 18

DAWN AT ISAWA IN THE KAI PROVINCE

1831–33, from Thirty-Six Views of Mount Fuji
Guimet Museum, Paris

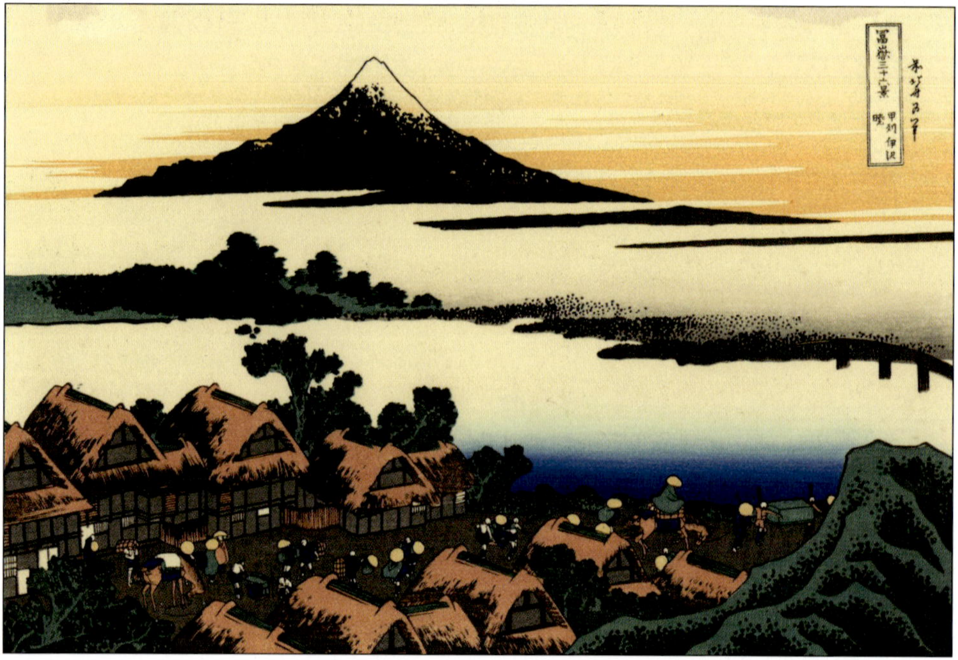

EJIRI IN THE SURUGA PROVINCE

1831–33, from Thirty-Six Views of Mount Fuji
Guimet Museum, Paris

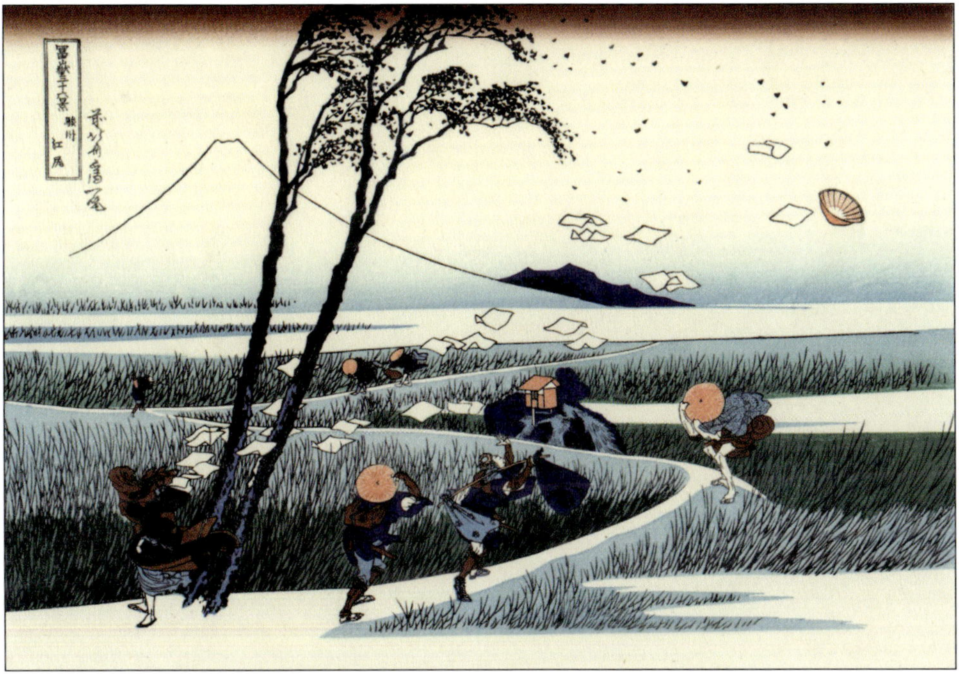

Plate 20

ENOSHIMA IN THE SAGAMI PROVINCE

1831–33, from Thirty-Six Views of Mount Fuji

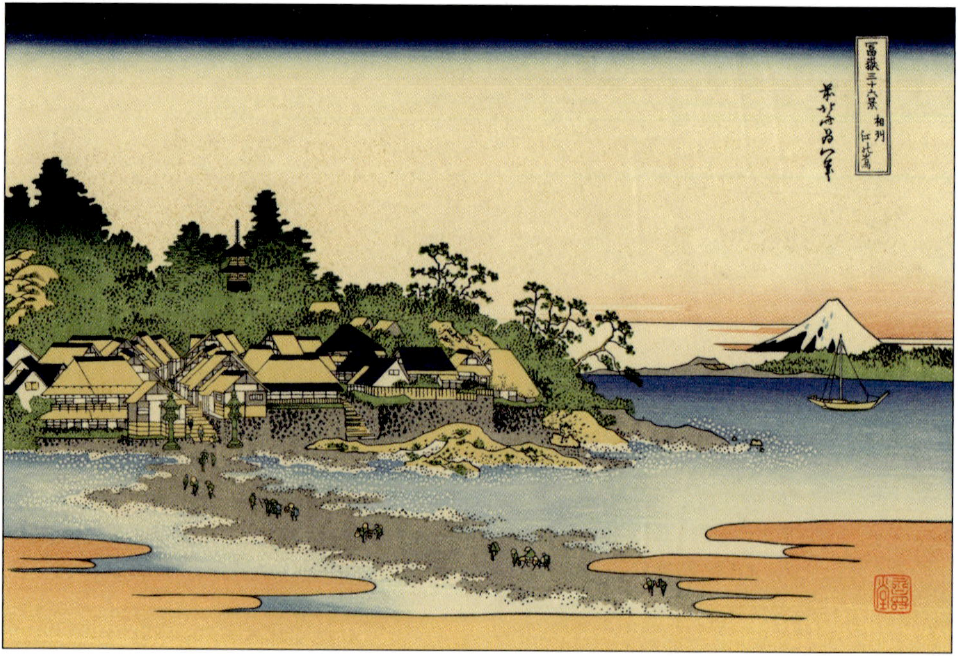

Plate 21

FUJI SEEN THROUGH THE MANNEN BRIDGE AT FUKAGAW

1831–33, from Thirty-Six Views of Mount Fuji

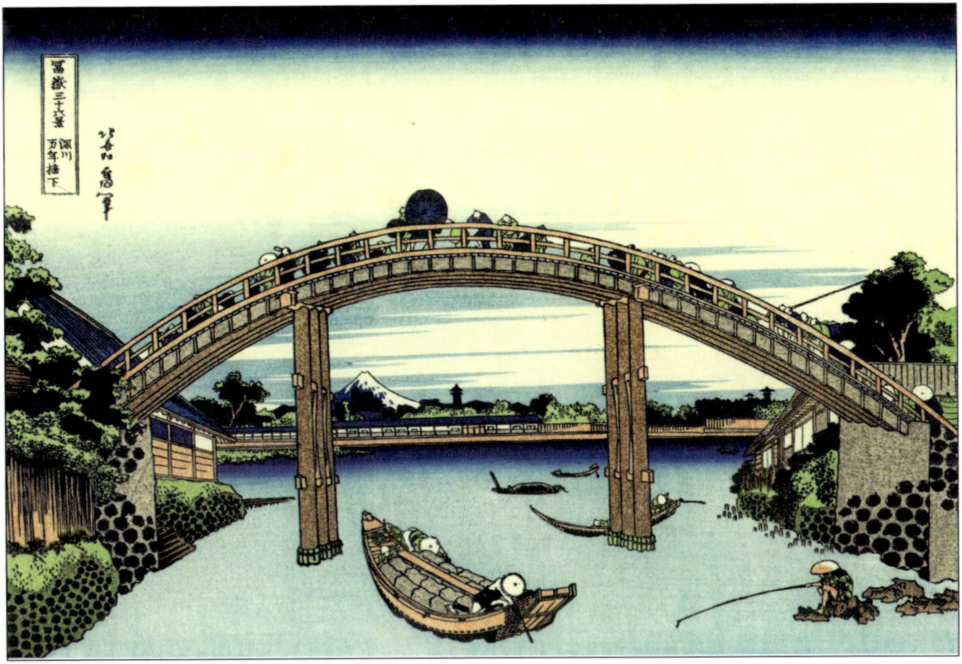

Plate 22

HODOGAYA ON THE TOKAIDO

1831–33, from Thirty-Six Views of Mount Fuji

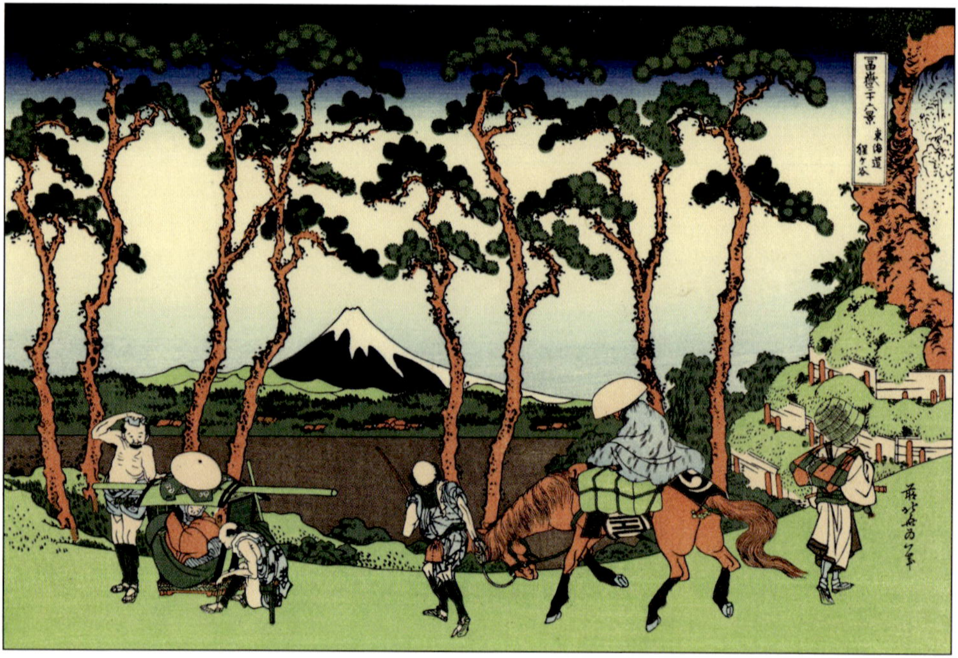

HONJO TATEKAWA, THE TIMBERYARD AT HONJO

1831–33, from Thirty-Six Views of Mount Fuji

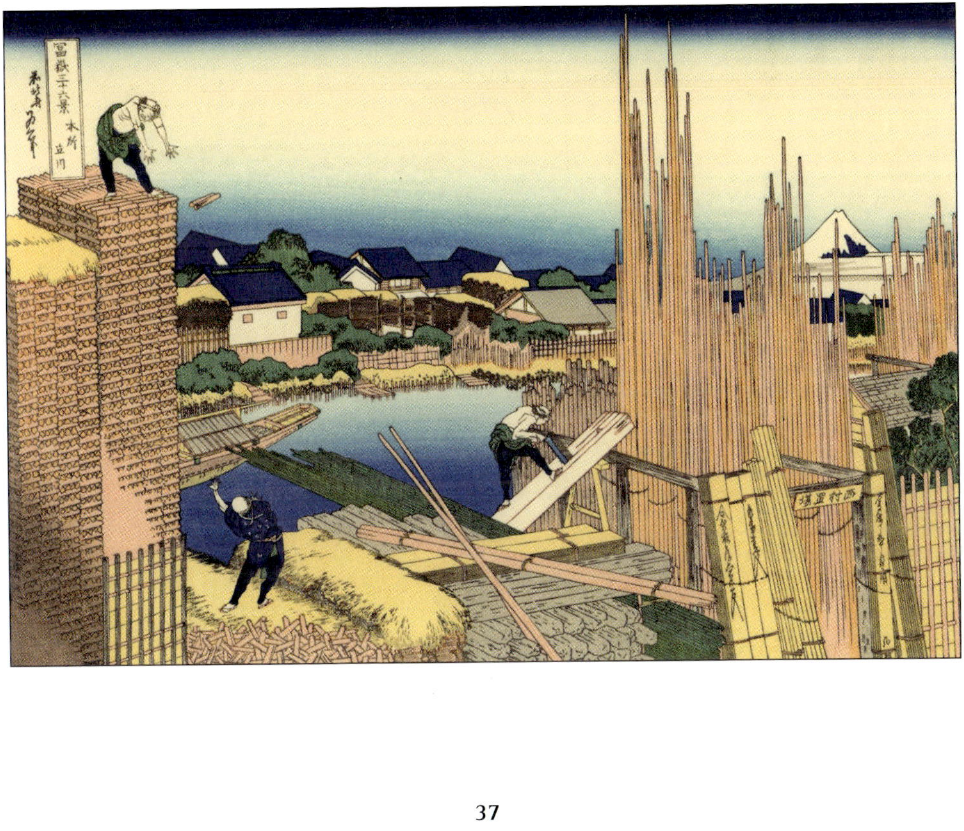

Plate 24

MITSUI SHOP ON SURUGA STREET IN EDO

1831–33, from Thirty-Six Views of Mount Fuji
Tokyo Fuji Art Museum

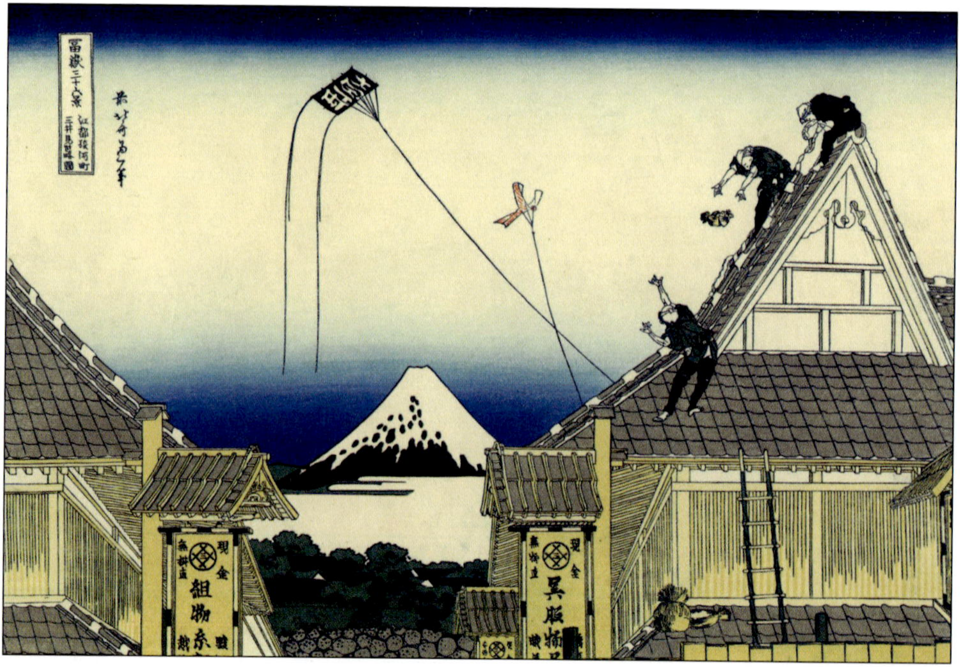

NAKAHARA IN THE SAGAMI PROVINCE

1831–33, from Thirty-Six Views of Mount Fuji
Guimet Museum, Paris

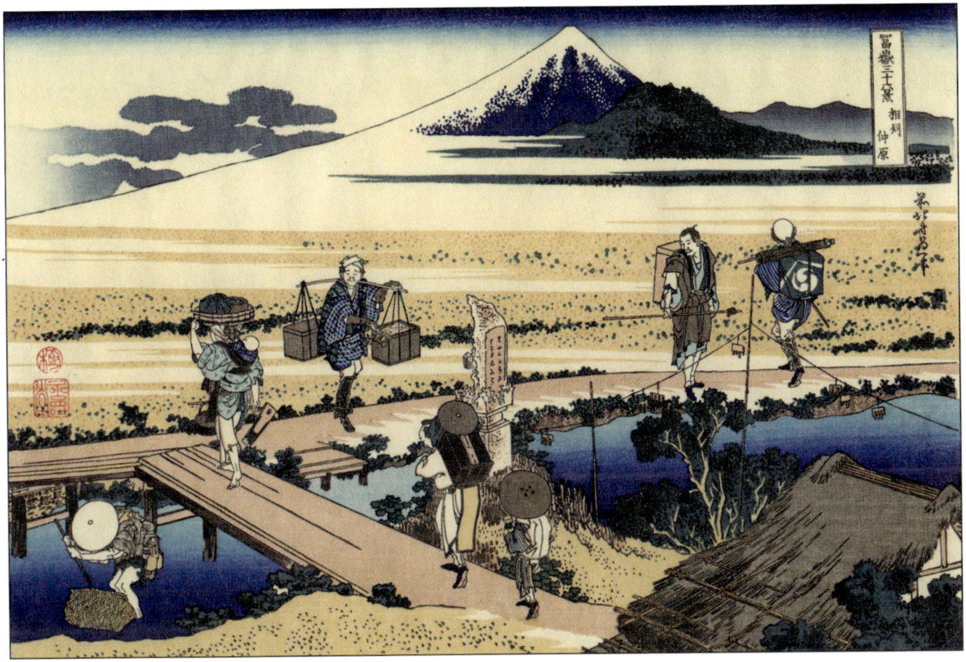

Plate 26

NIHONBASHI BRIDGE IN EDO

1831–33, from Thirty-Six Views of Mount Fuji

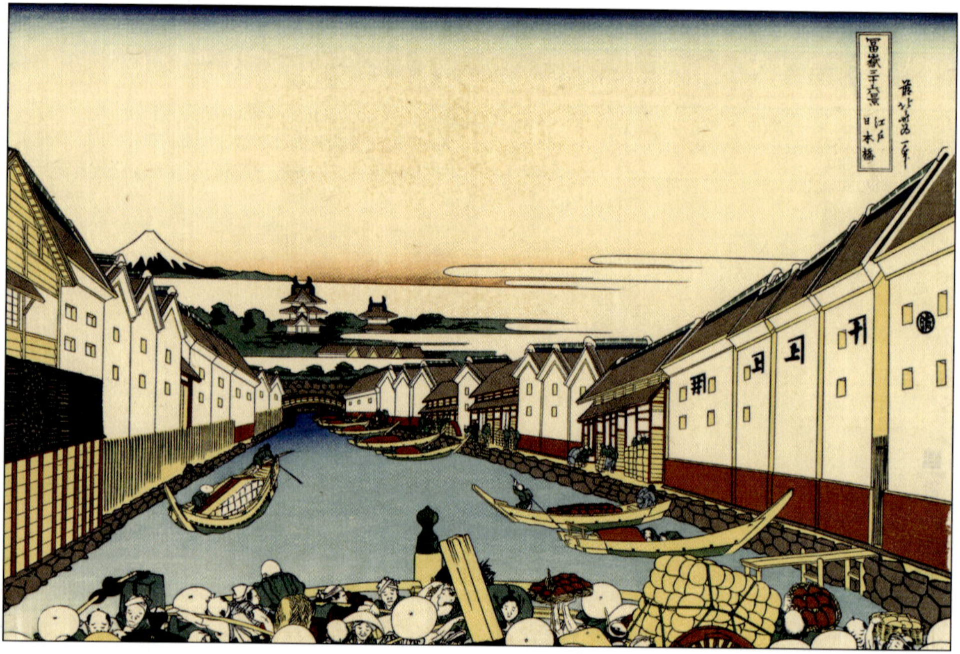

Plate 27

SHIMOMEGURO

1831–33, from Thirty-Six Views of Mount Fuji

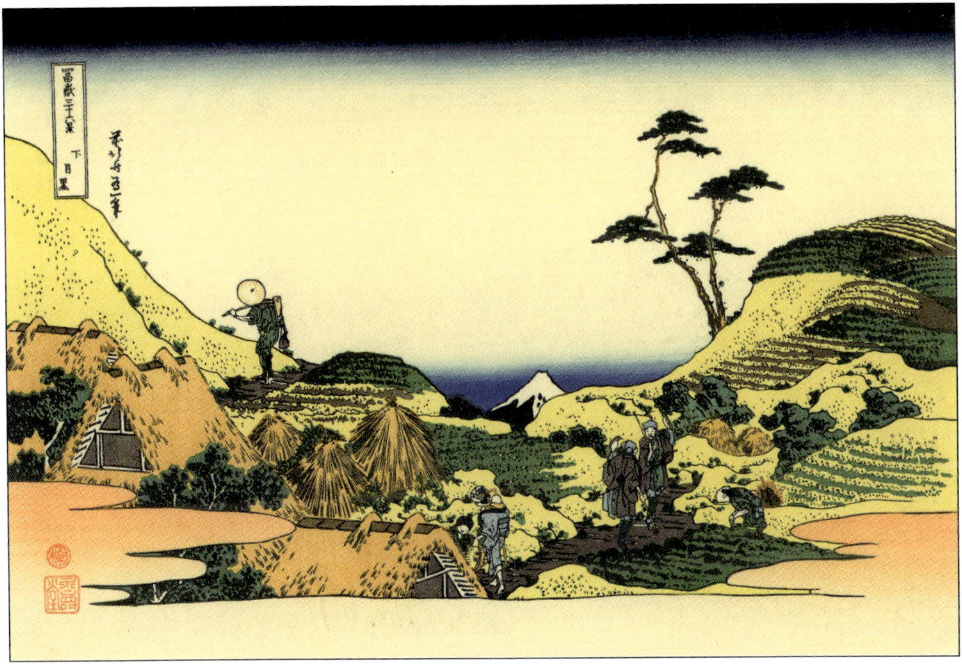

Plate 28

SENJU IN THE MUSACHI PROVINCE

1831–33, from Thirty-Six Views of Mount Fuji

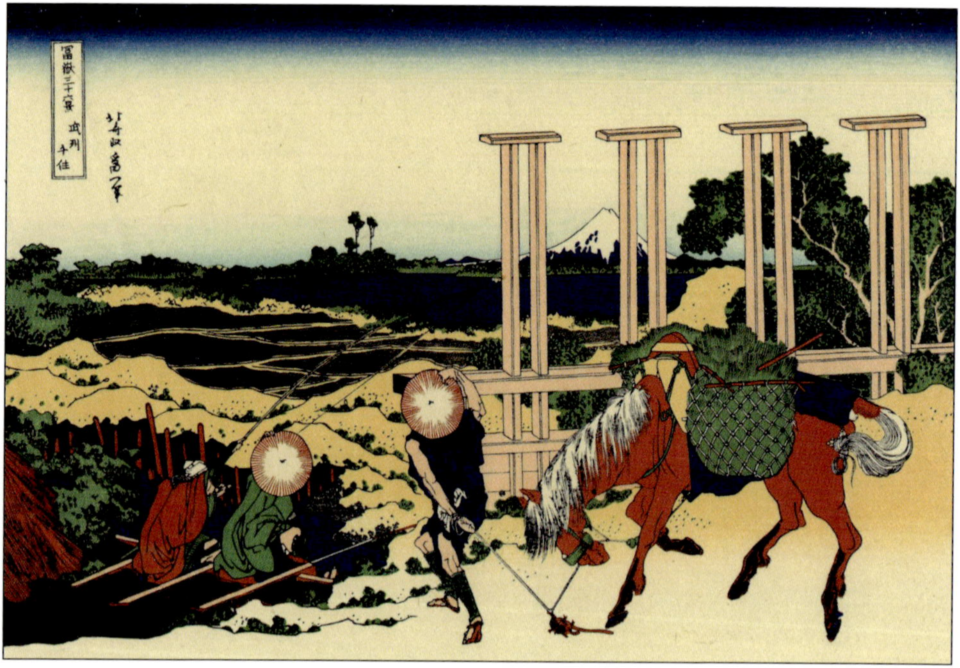

SHORE OF TAGO BAY, EJIRI AT TOKAIDO

1831–33, from Thirty-Six Views of Mount Fuji

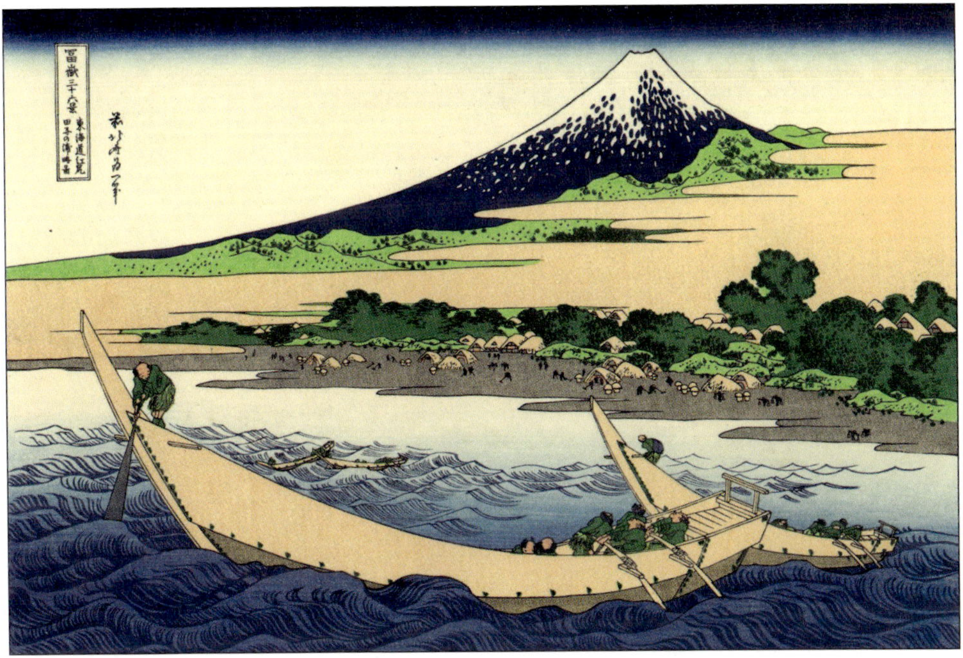

Plate 30

THE FIELDS OF SEKIYA BY THE SUMIDA RIVER

1831–33, from Thirty-Six Views of Mount Fuji
The British Library, London

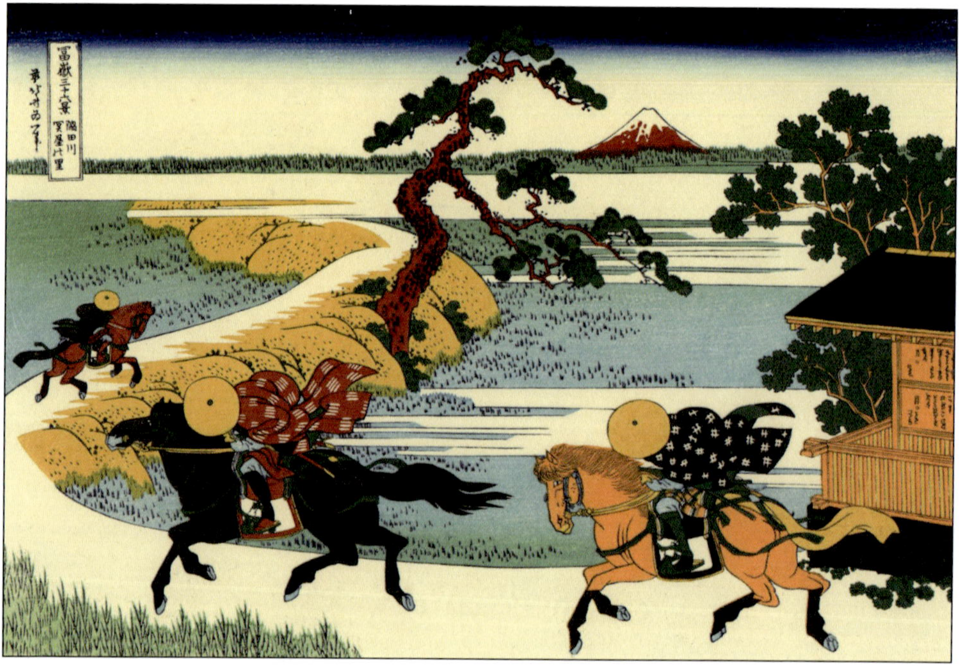

USHIBORI IN THE HITACHI PROVINCE

1831–33, from Thirty-Six Views of Mount Fuji

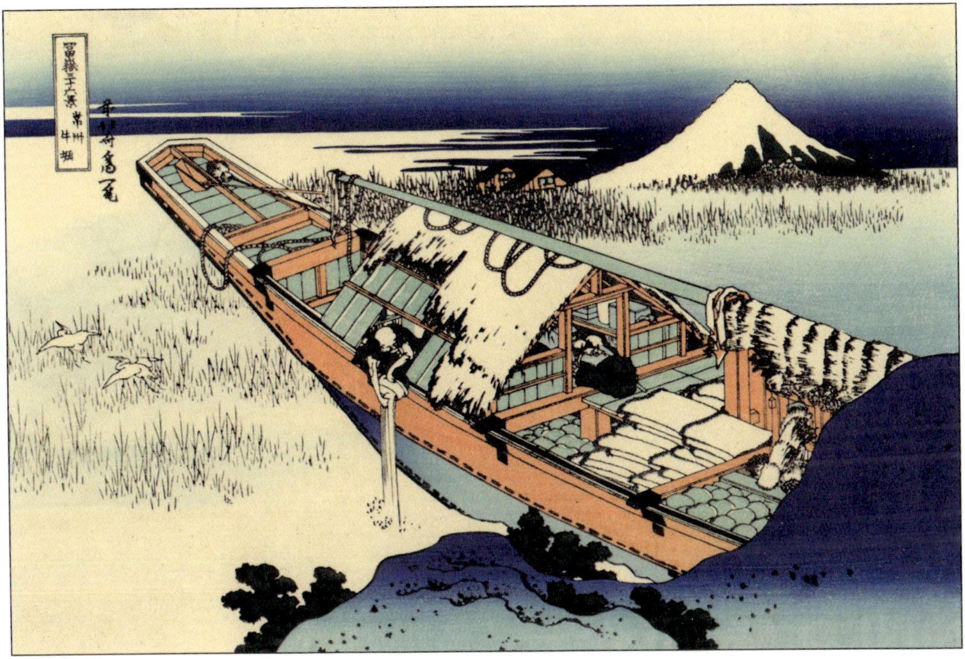

Plate 32

WATERMILL AT ONDEN

1831–33, from Thirty-Six Views of Mount Fuji

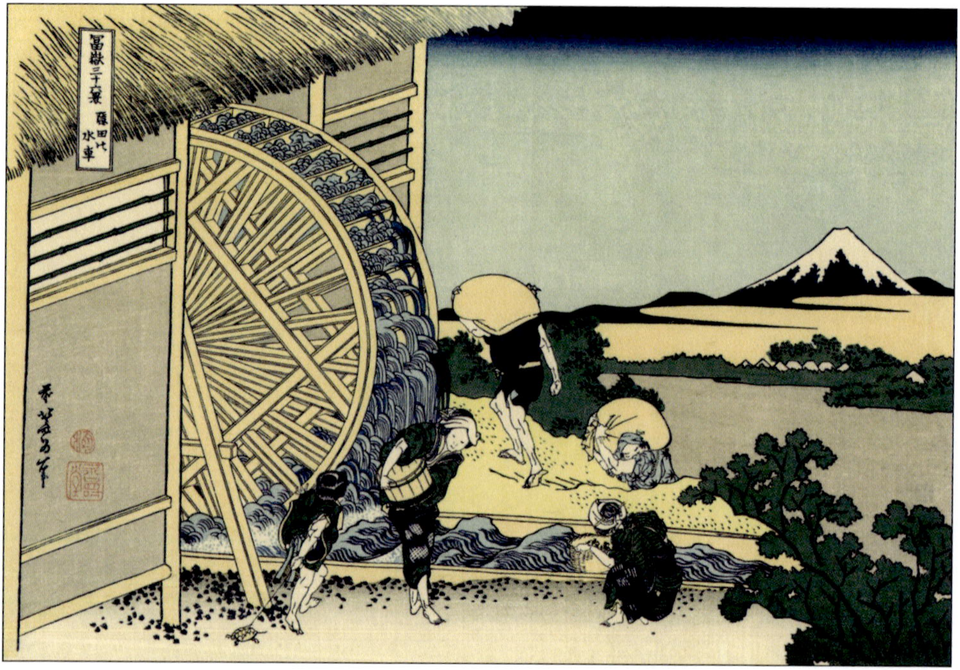

INUME PASS IN THE KAI PROVINCE

1831–33, from Thirty-Six Views of Mount Fuji

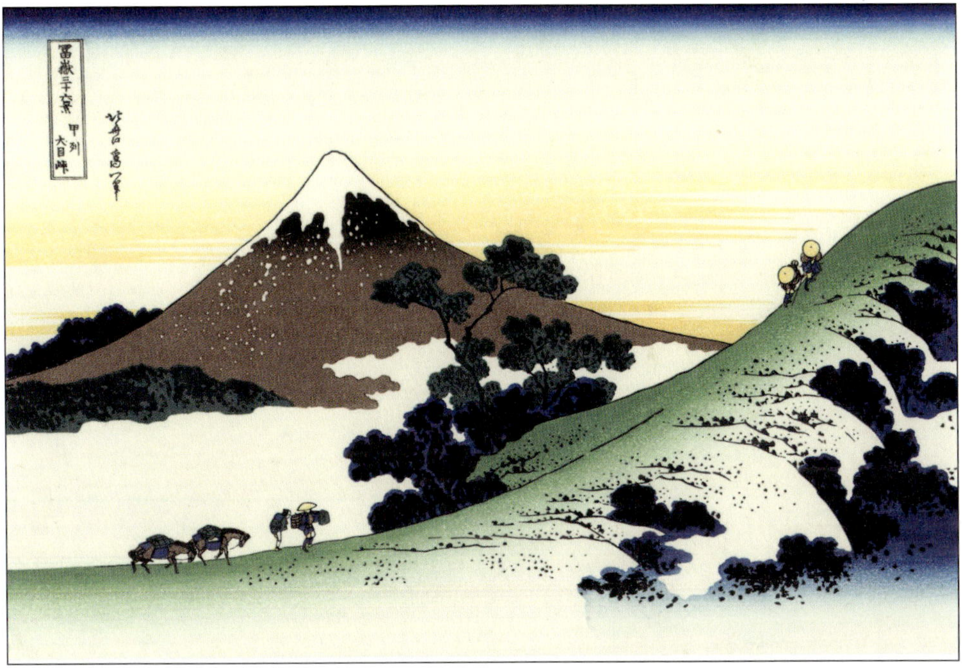

Plate 34

KAJIKAZAWA IN THE KAI PROVINCE

1831–33, from Thirty-Six Views of Mount Fuji

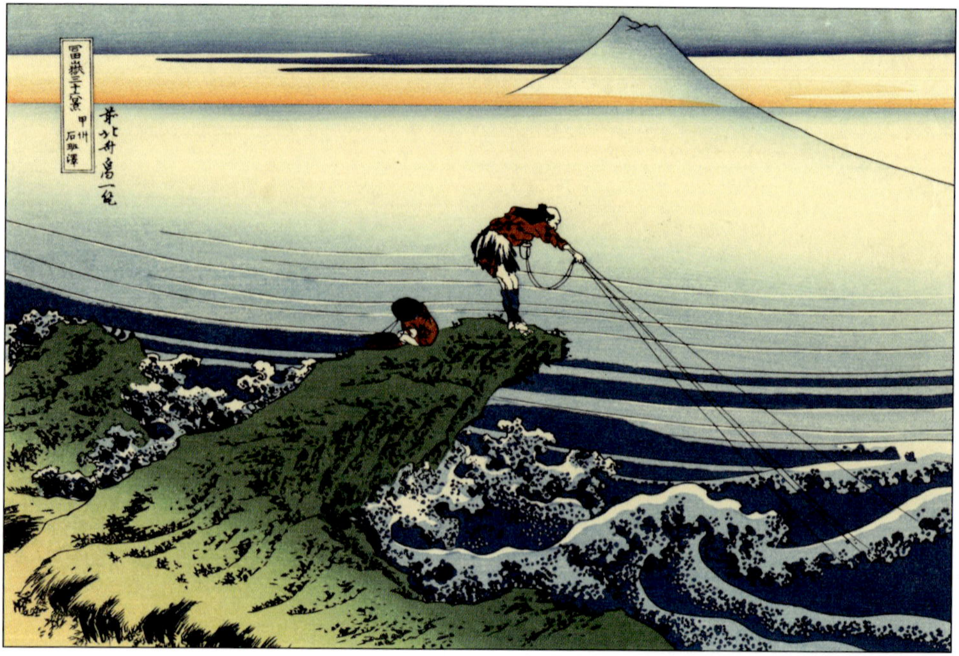

LAKE SUWA IN THE SHINANO PROVINCE

1831–33, from Thirty-Six Views of Mount Fuji
Guiment Museum, Paris

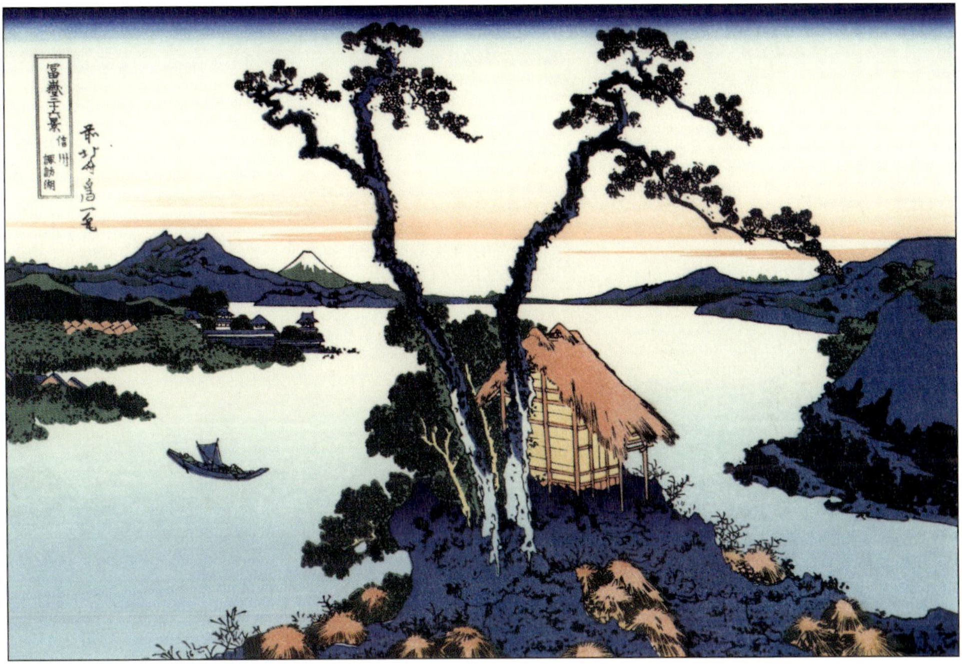

Plate 36

THE KAZUSA SEA ROUTE

1831–33, from Thirty-Six Views of Mount Fuji

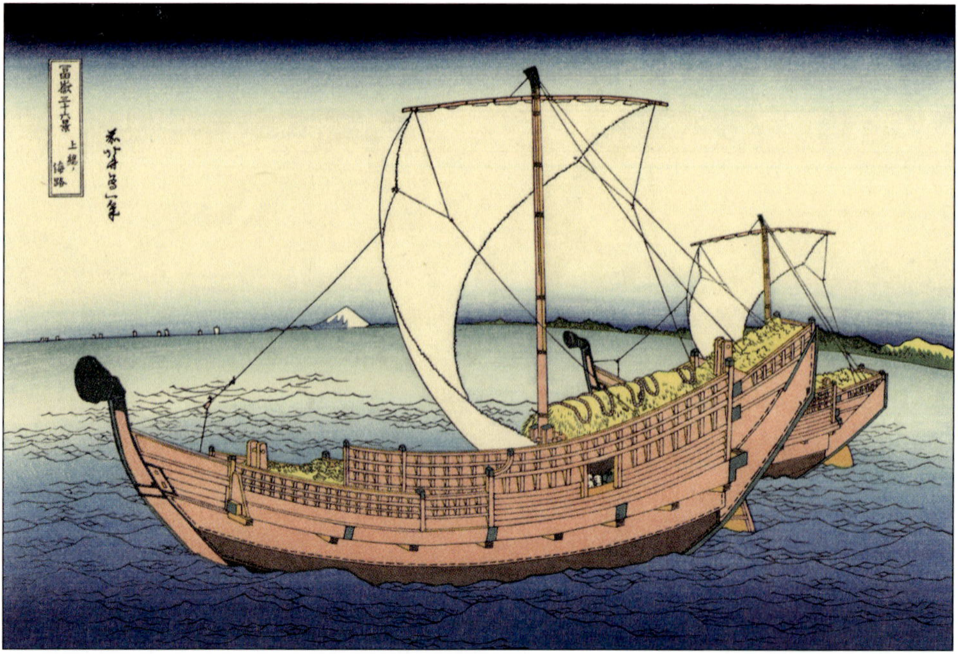

SHICHIRI BEACH IN SAGAMI PROVINCE

1831–33, from Thirty-Six Views of Mount Fuji

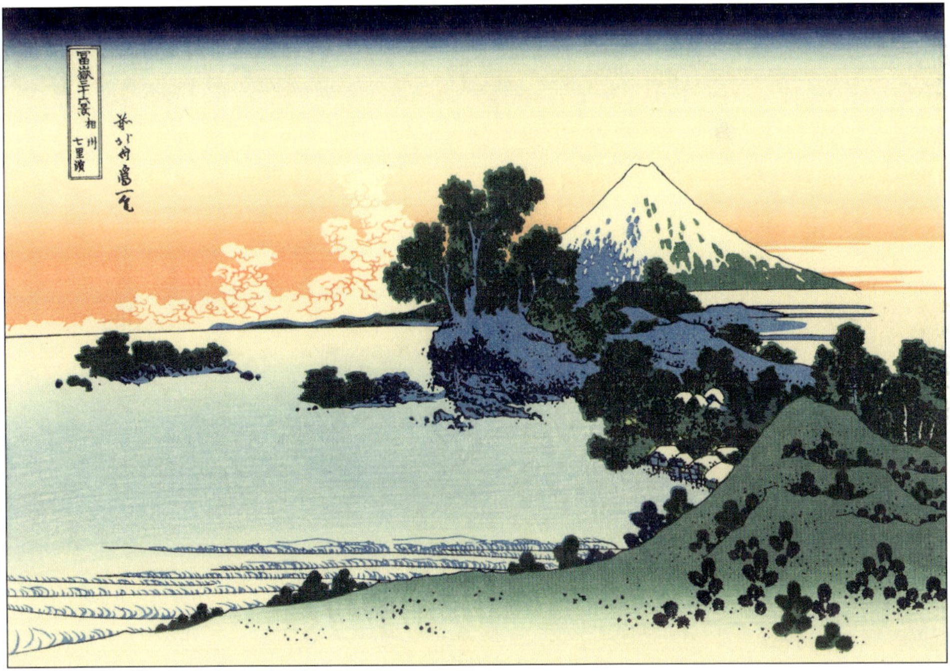

Plate 38

SUNSET ACROSS THE RYOGOKU BRIDGE FROM THE BANK OF THE SUMIDA RIVER AT ONMAGAYASHI

1831–33, from Thirty-Six Views of Mount Fuji

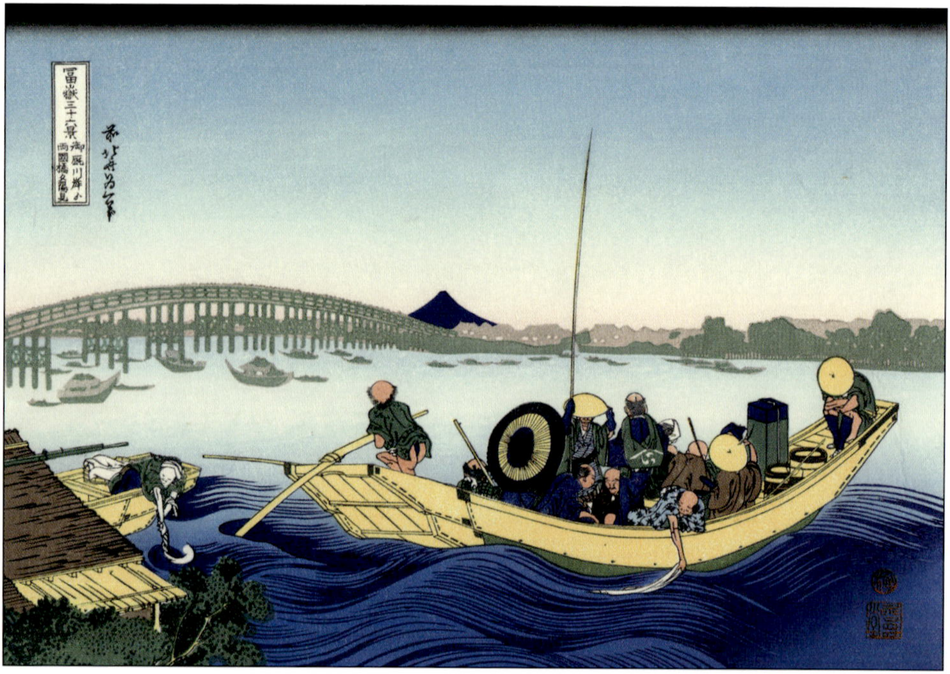

TAMA RIVER IN THE MUSASHI PROVINCE

1831–33, from Thirty-Six Views of Mount Fuji

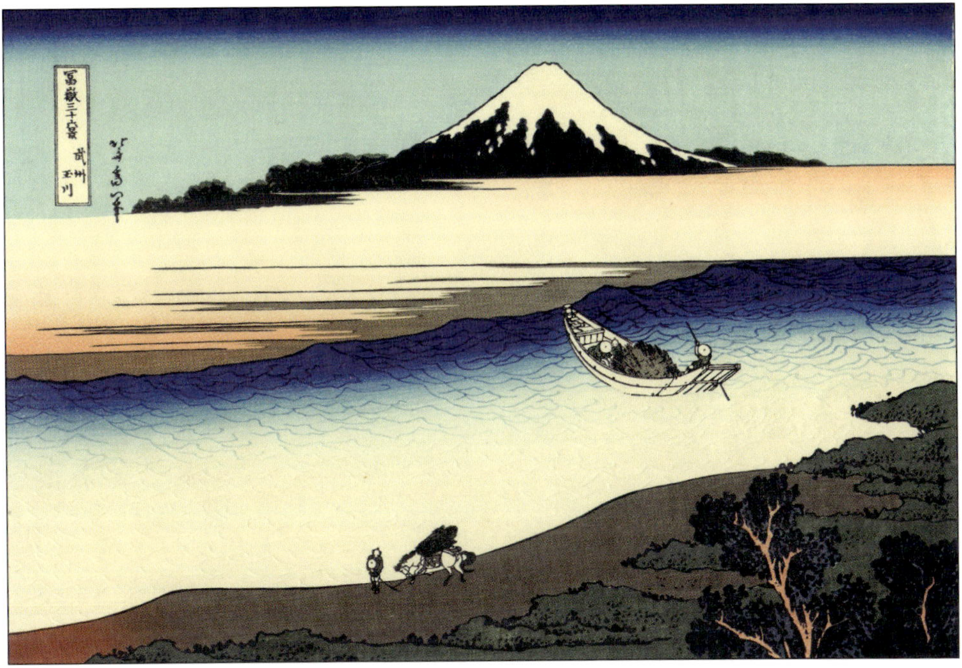

Plate 40

TEA HOUSE AT KOISHIKAWA THE MORNING AFTER A SNOWFALL

1831–33, from Thirty-Six Views of Mount Fuji

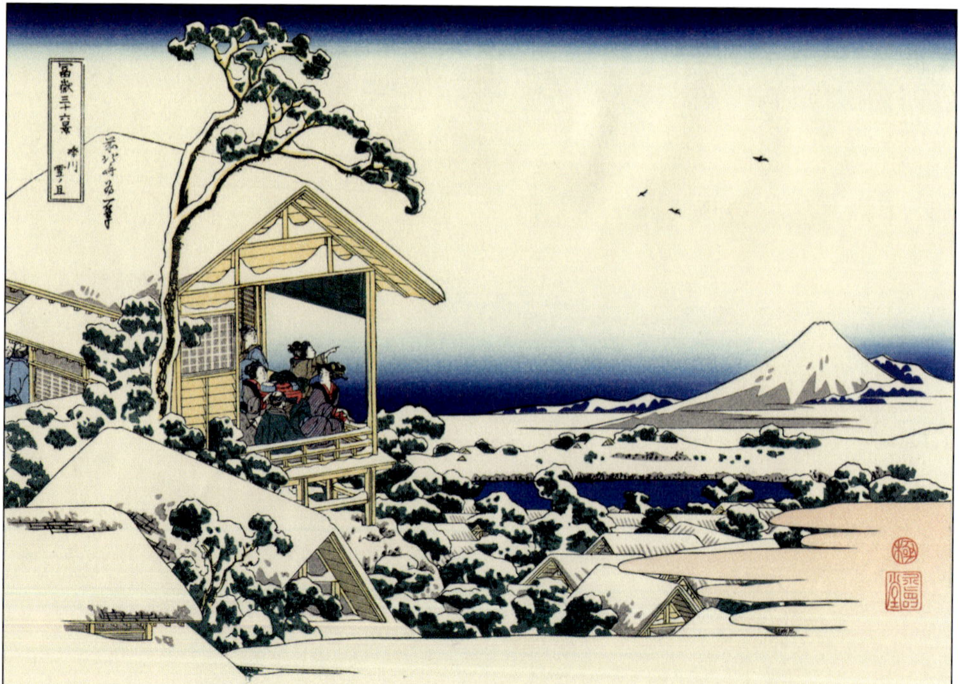

THE BACK OF MOUNT FUJI FROM THE MINOBU RIVER

1831–33, from Thirty-Six Views of Mount Fuji

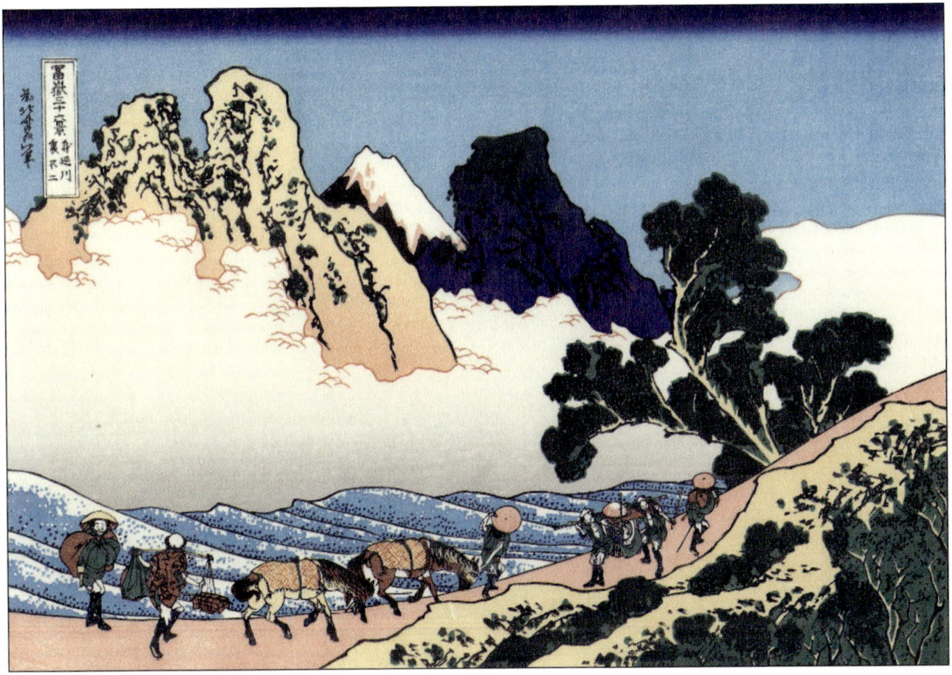

Plate 42

MOUNT FUJI FROM KANAYA ON THE TOKAIDO

1831–33, from Thirty-Six Views of Mount Fuji

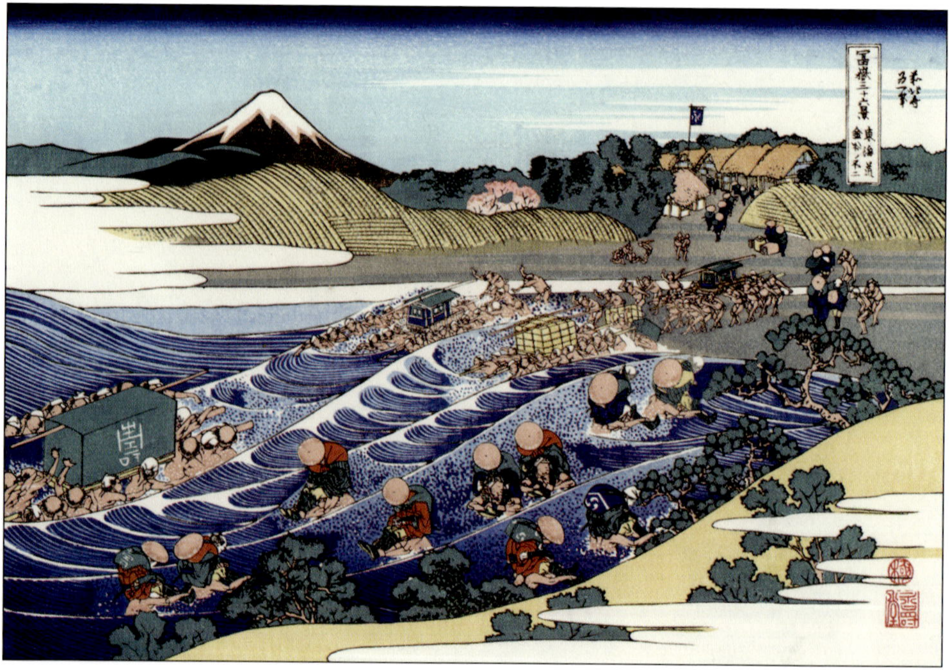

MOUNT FUJI REFLECTS IN LAKE KAWAGUCHI SEEN FROM THE MISAKA PASS IN THE KAI PROVINCE

1831–33, from Thirty-Six Views of Mount Fuji

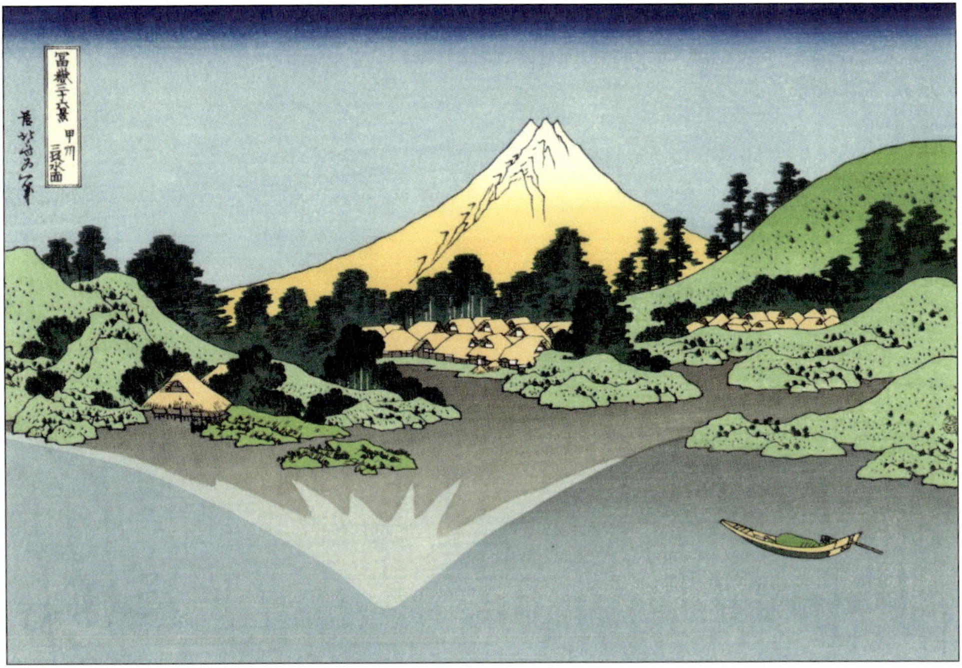

Plate 44

SUNDAI, EDO

1831–33, from Thirty-Six Views of Mount Fuji

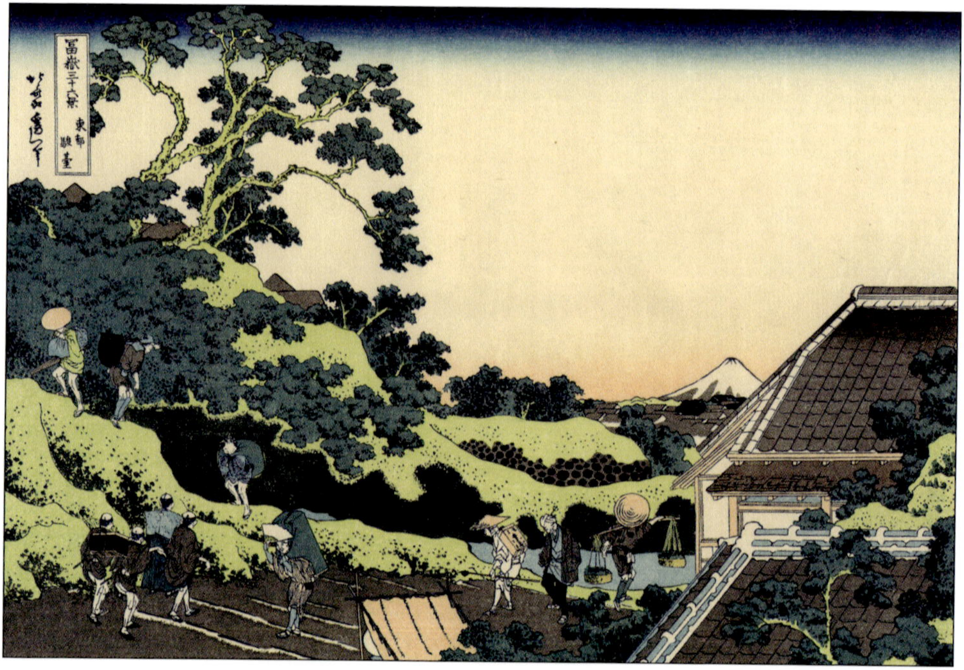

LAKE OF HAKONE IN THE SEGAMI PROVINCE

1831–33, from Thirty-Six Views of Mount Fuji

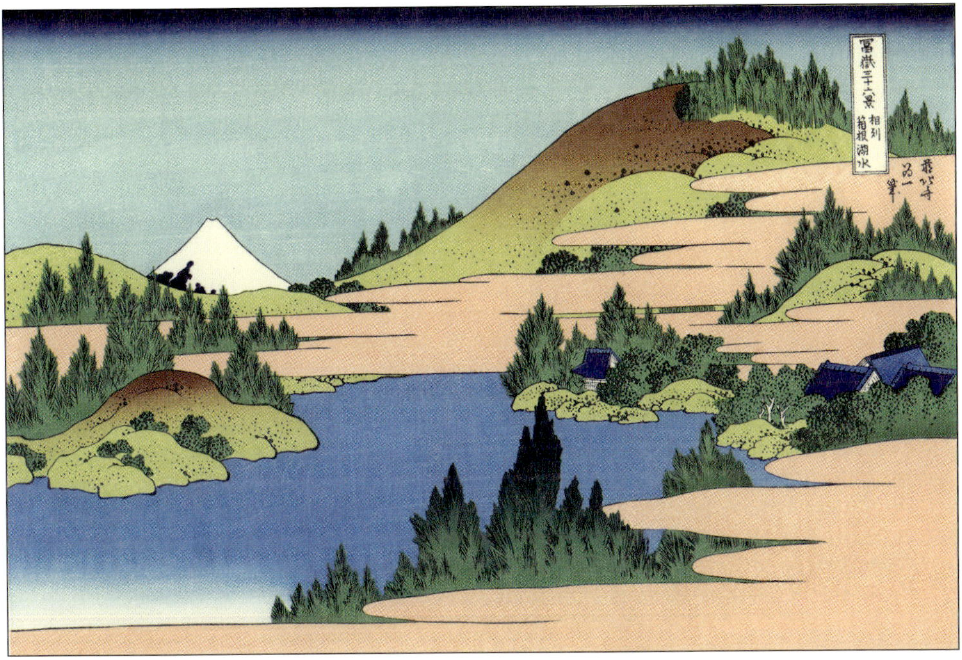

Plate 46

THE TEA PLANTATION OF KATAKURA IN THE SURUGA PROVINCE

1831–33, from Thirty-Six Views of Mount Fuji

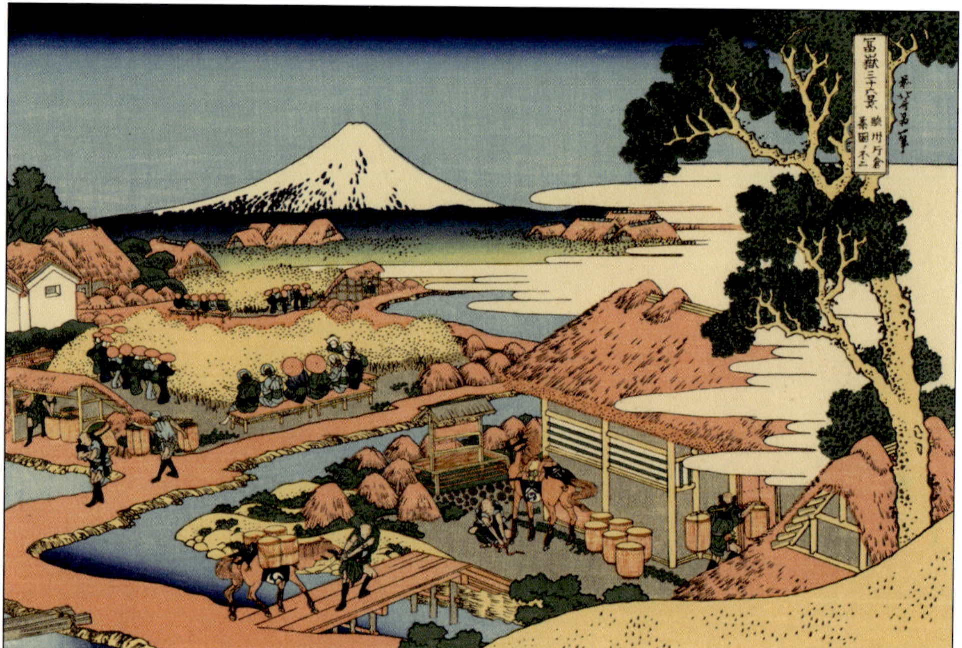

TSUKADA ISLAND IN THE MUSASHI PROVINCE

Plate 47

1831–33, from Thirty-Six Views of Mount Fuji

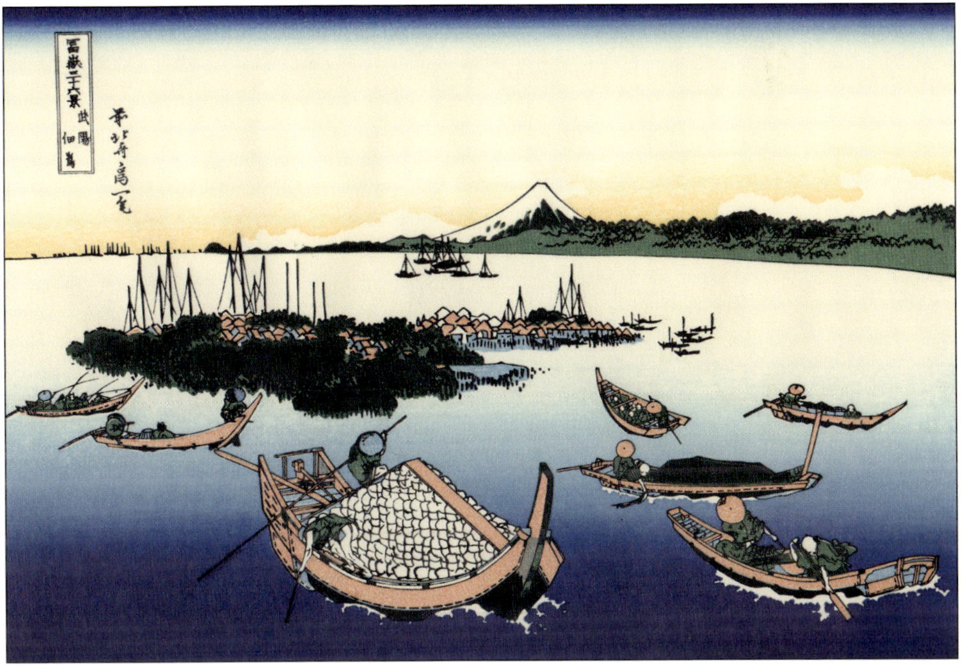

UMEGAWA IN SAGAMI PROVINCE

1831–33, from Thirty-Six Views of Mount Fuji

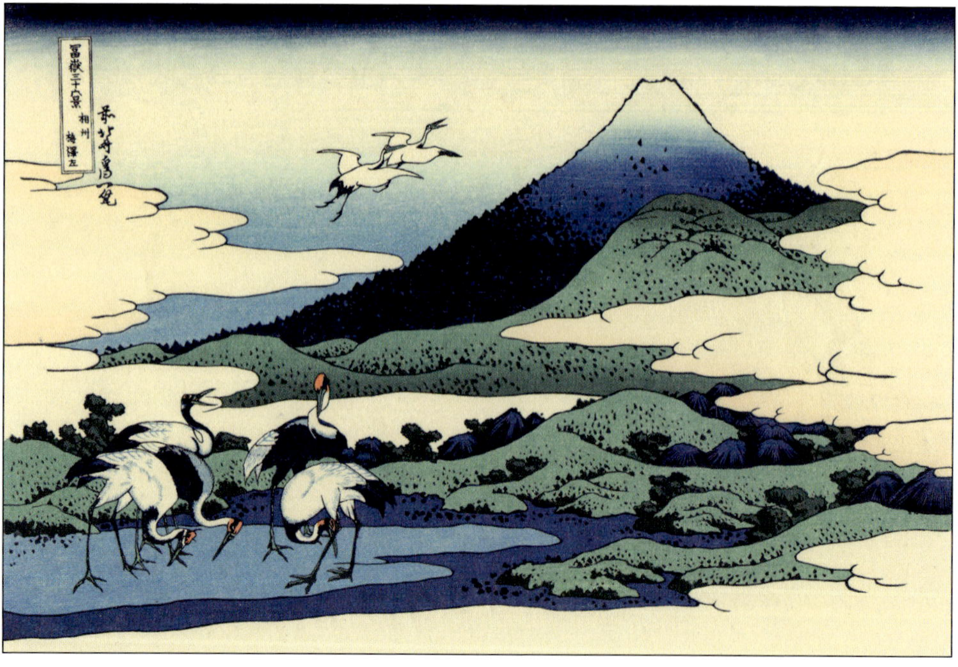

YOSHIDA AT TOKAIDO

1831–33, from Thirty-Six Views of Mount Fuji

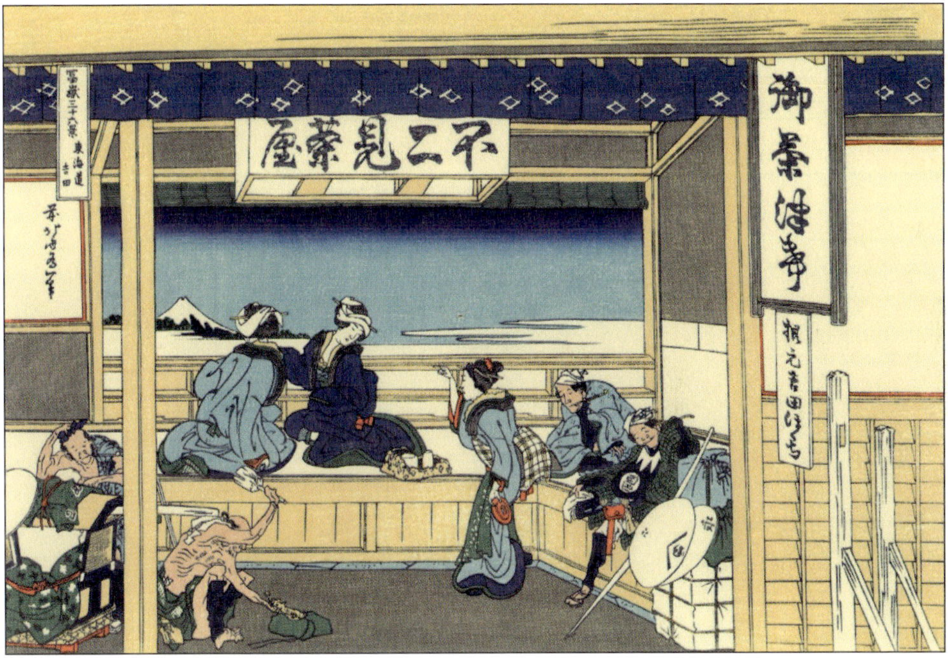

Plate 50

PORTRAIT OF CHINO HYOGO SEATED AT HIS WRITING DESK

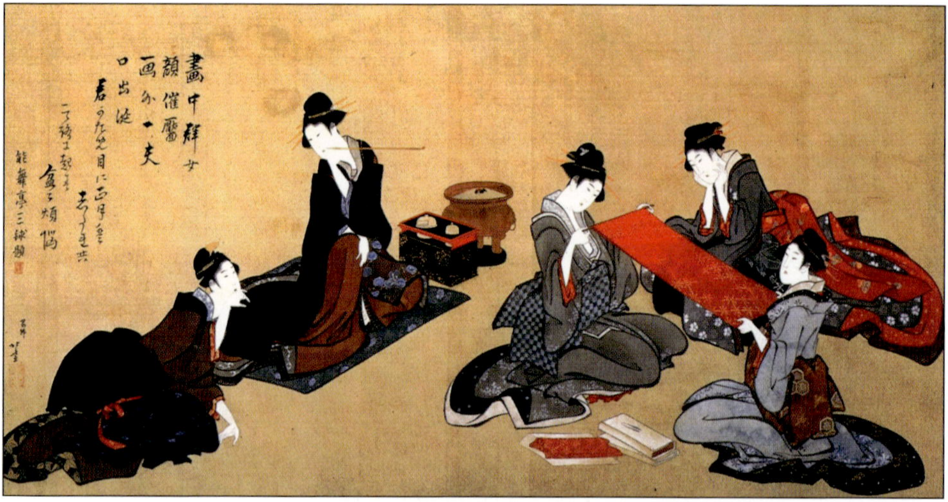

A WOMAN GHOST APPEARED FROM A WELL

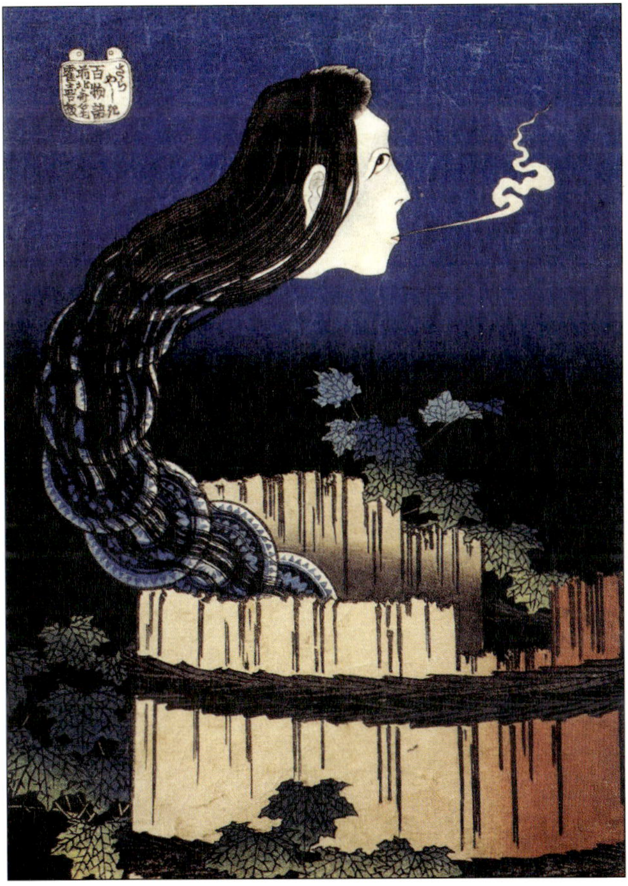

OIRAN AND KAMURO

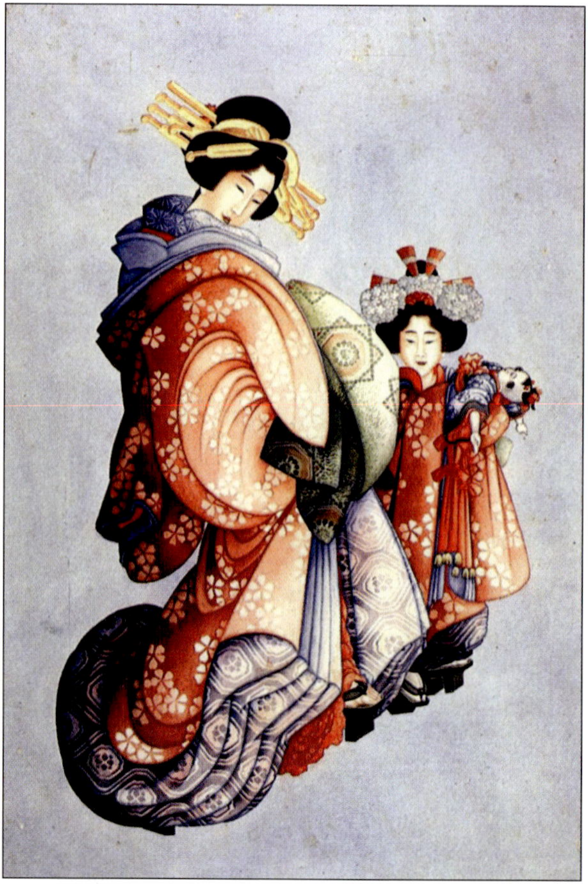

A LEATHER POUCH WITH KAGAMI

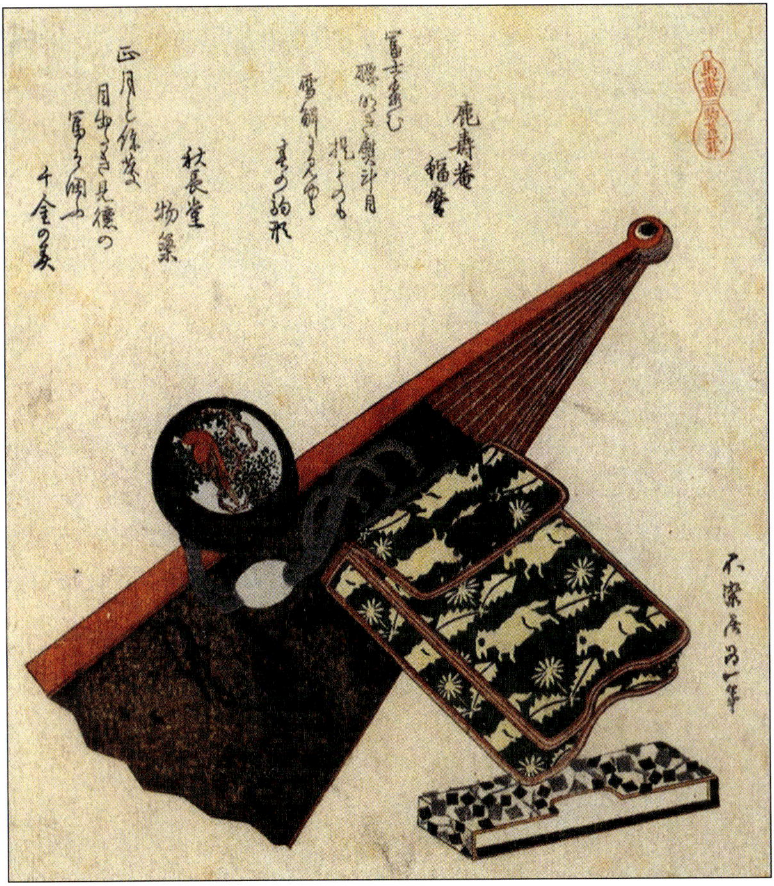

Plate 54

PORTRAIT OF A WOMAN

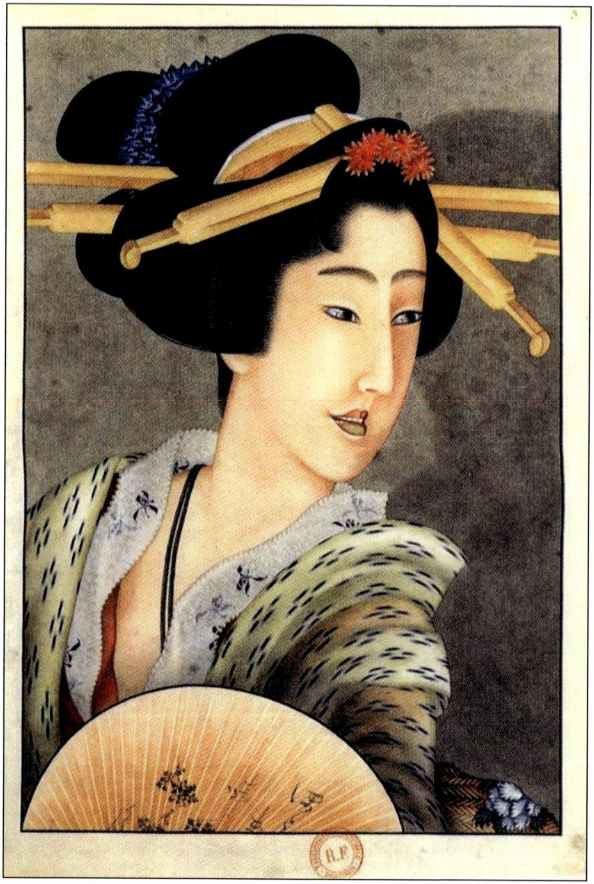

PORTRAIT OF A MAN

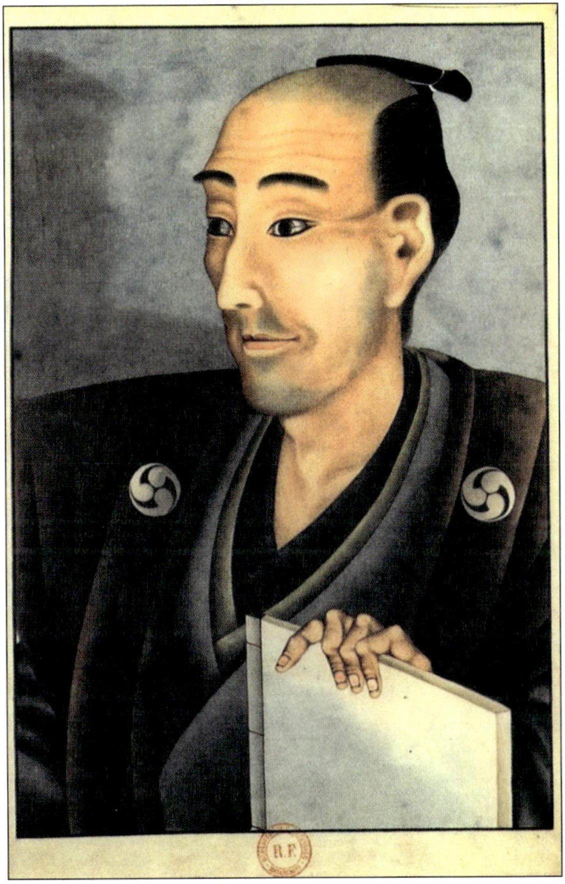

Plate 56

CARP LEAPING UP A CASCADE

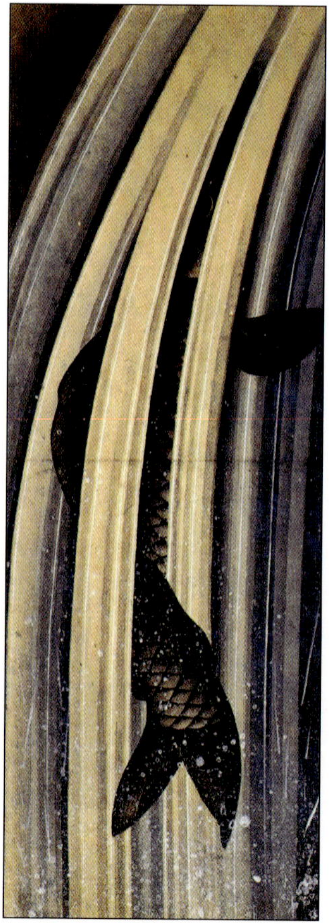

POPPIES

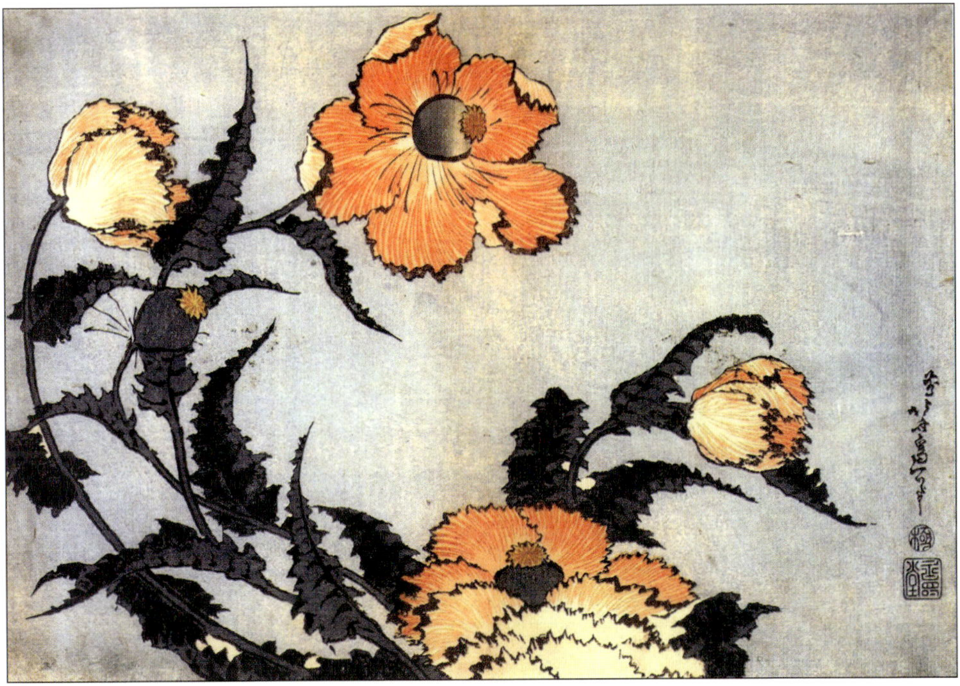

Plate 58

FIVE FANS

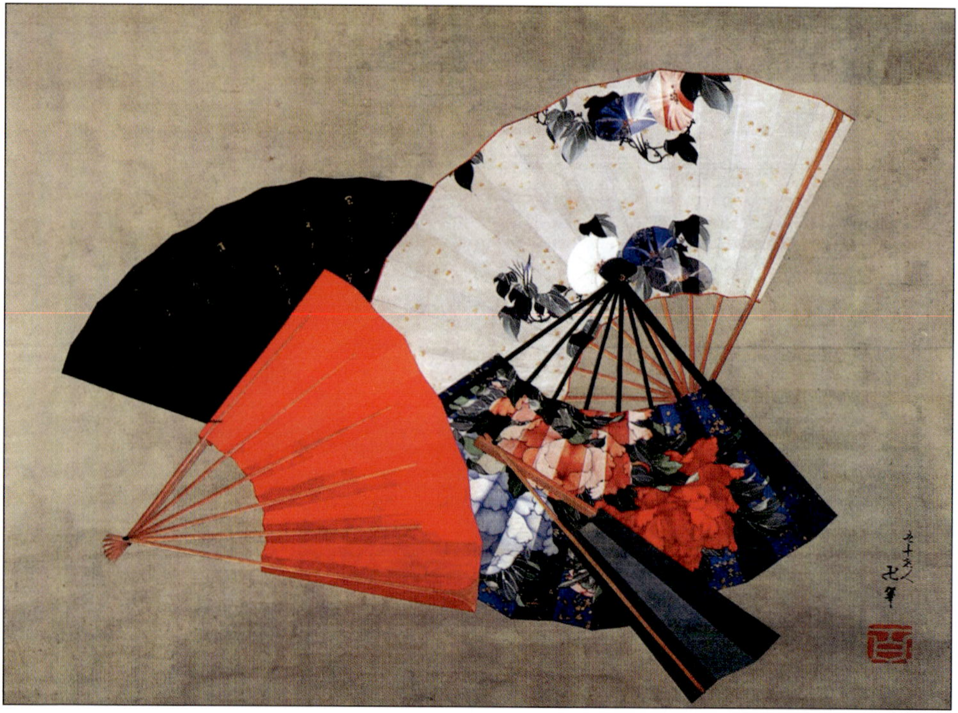

PORCELAIN POT WITH OPEN FAN

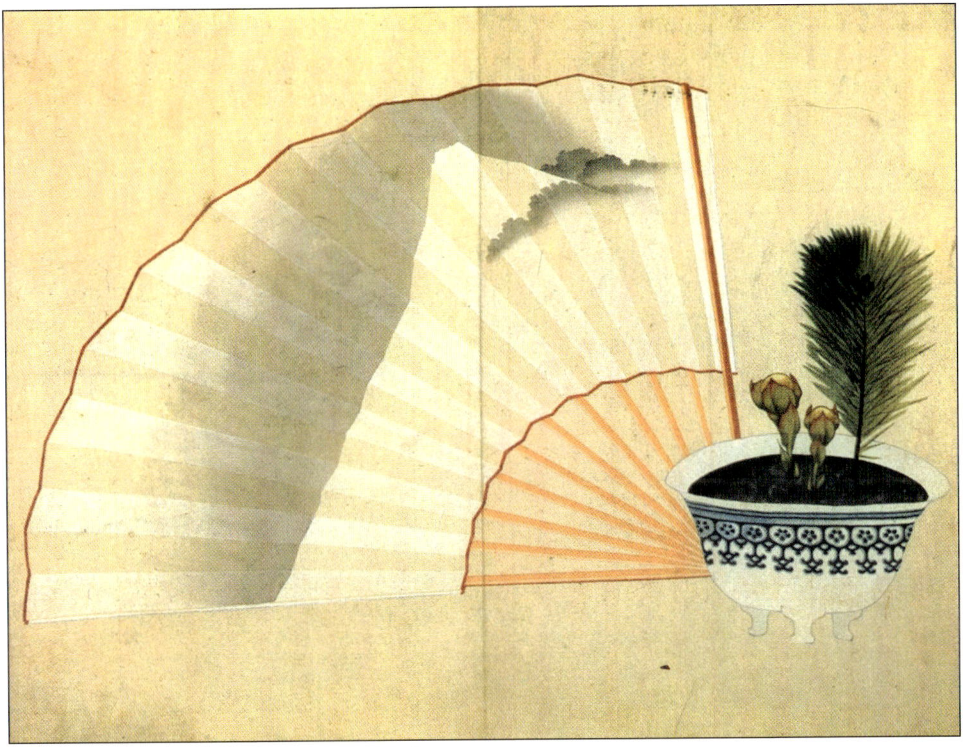

Plate 60

PHOENIX

On the ceiling of the Ganshoin Temple at Obuse

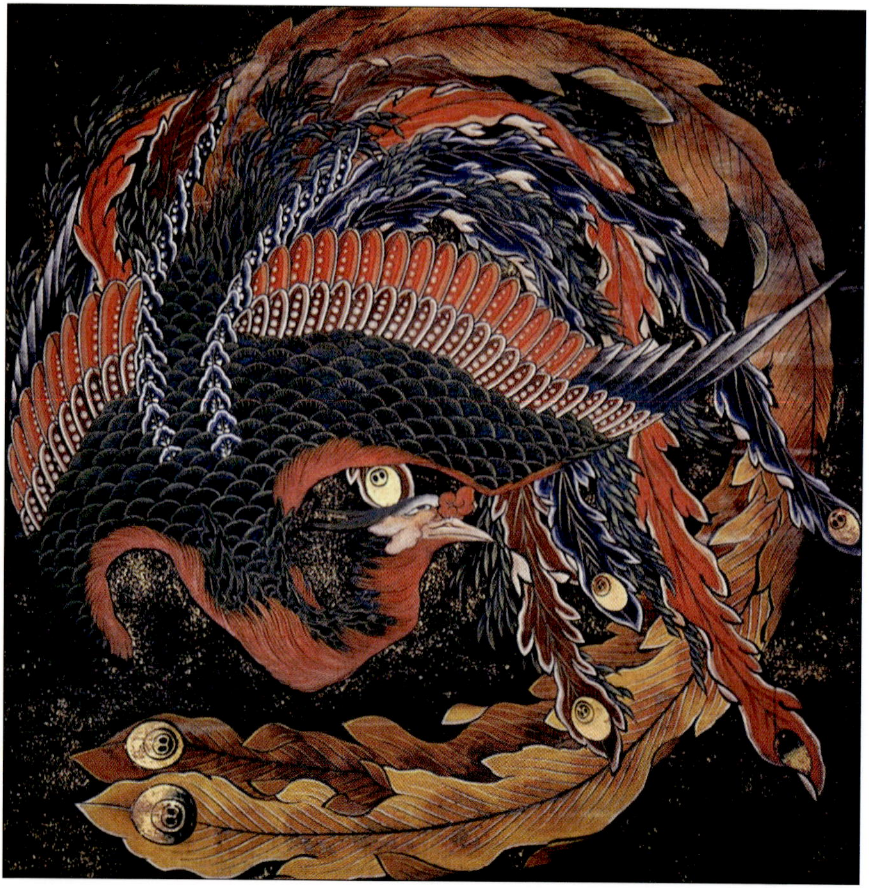

DRAGON

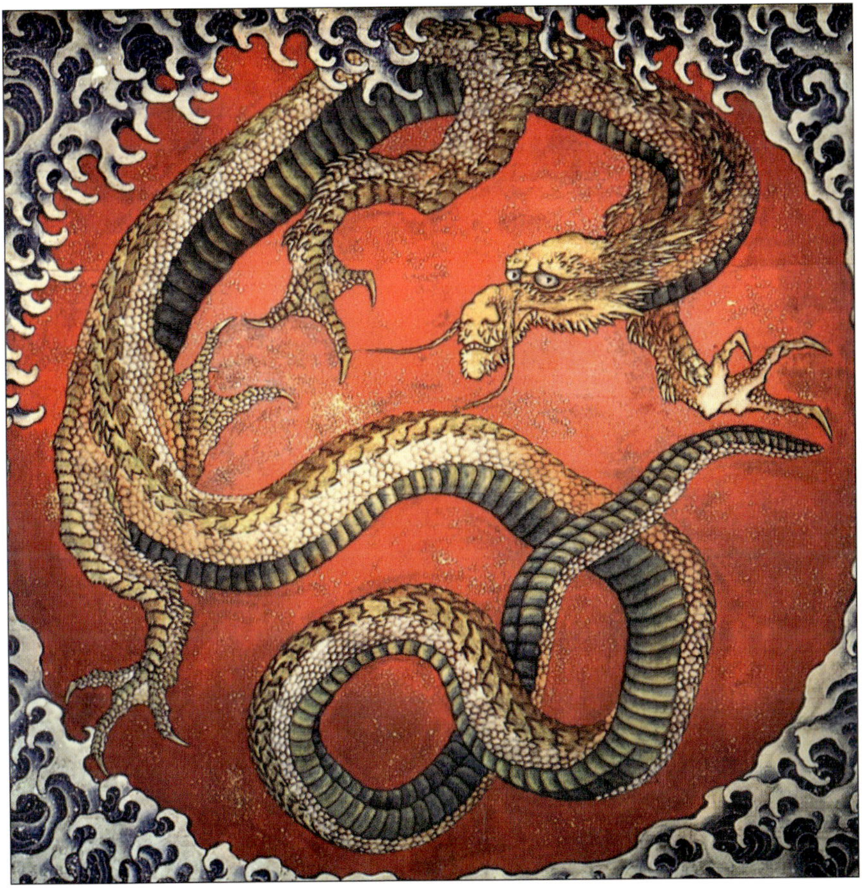

Plate 62

A MERCHANT MAKING UP THE ACCOUNT

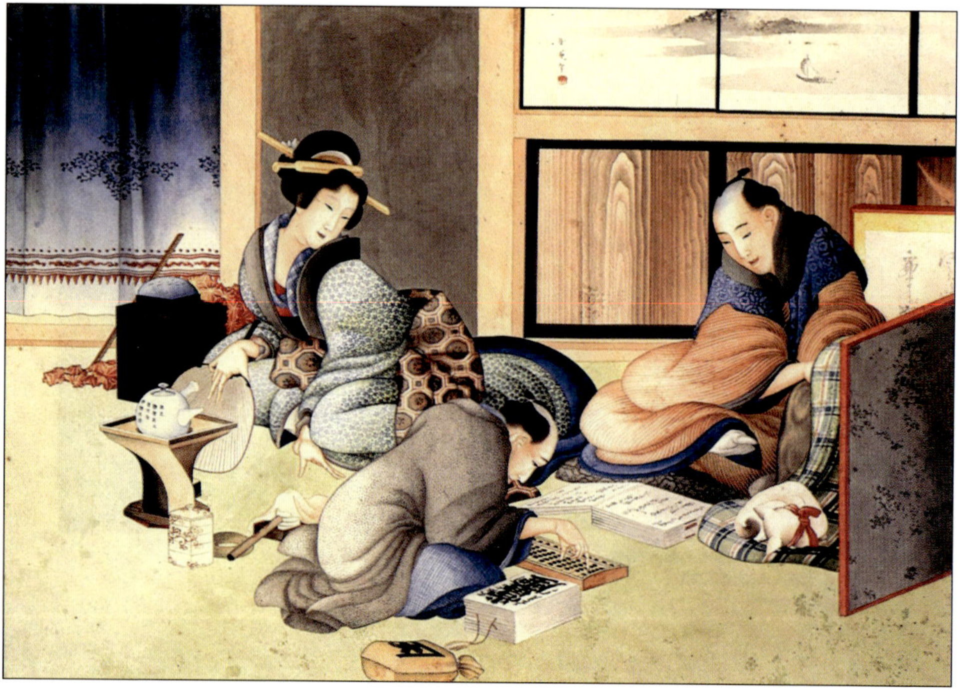

HAWK ON A CEREMONIAL STAND

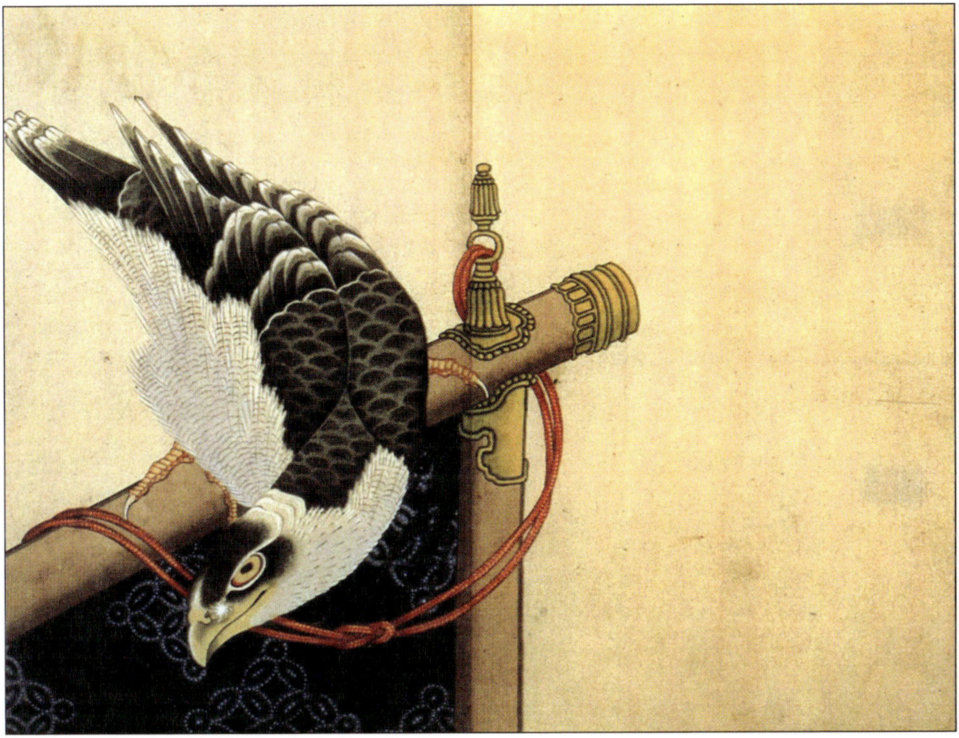

Plate 64

A BOWL OF LIP ROUGE

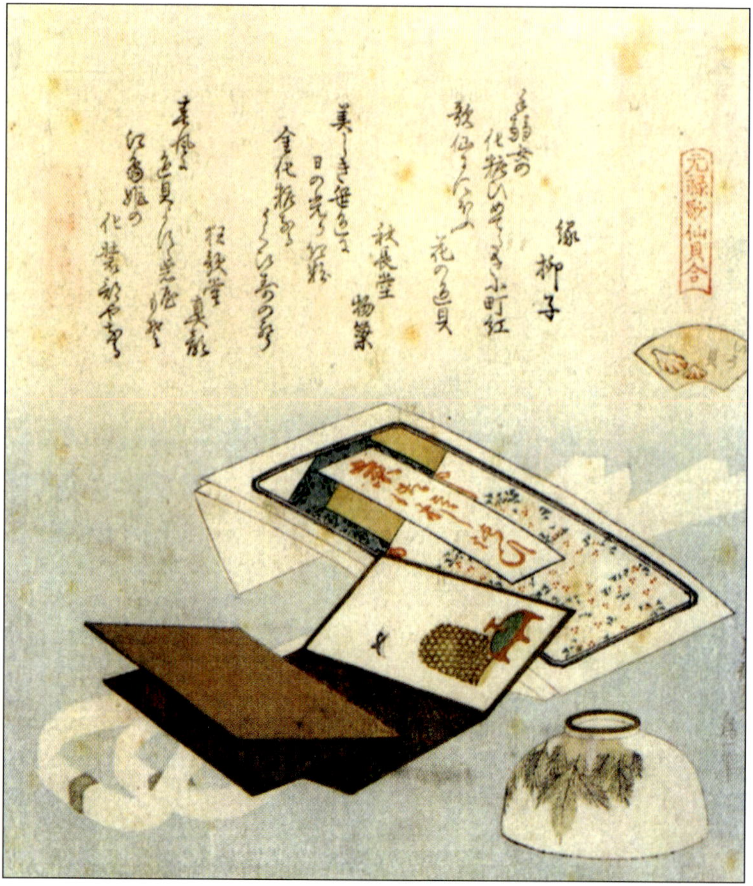

A LACQUERED WASHBASIN AND EWER

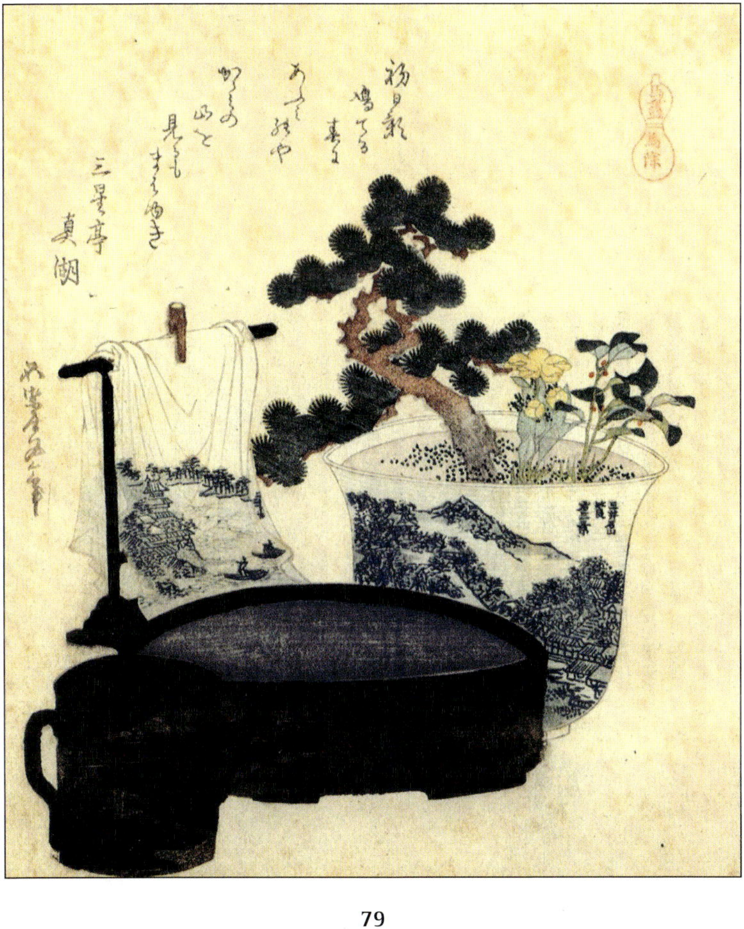

Plate 66

MASCULINE WAVE

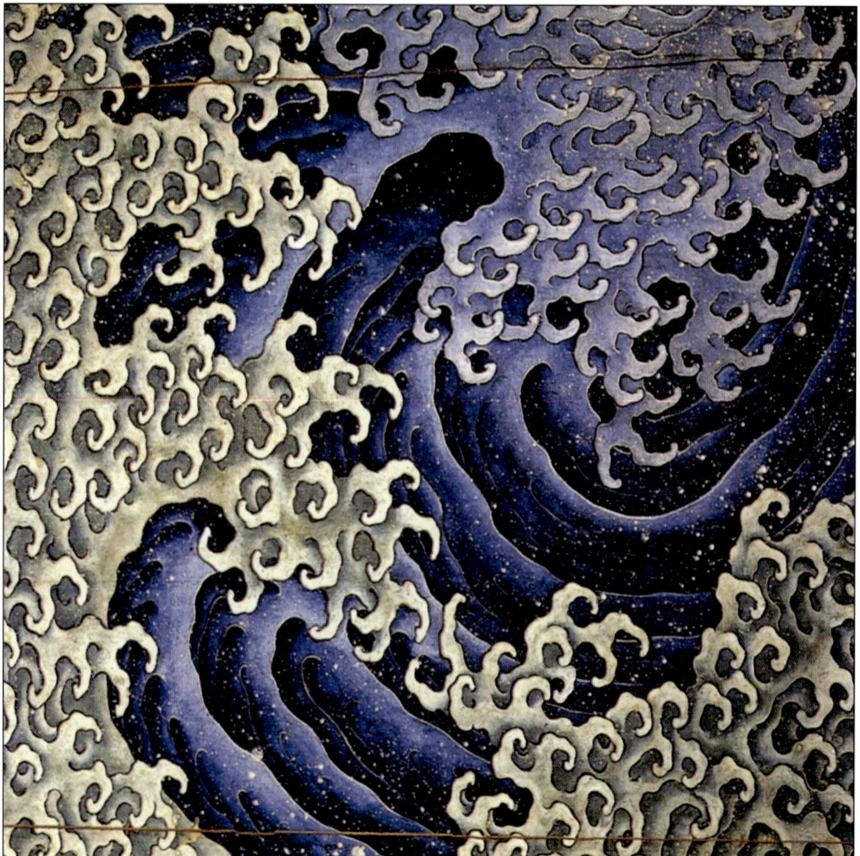

FEMININE WAVE

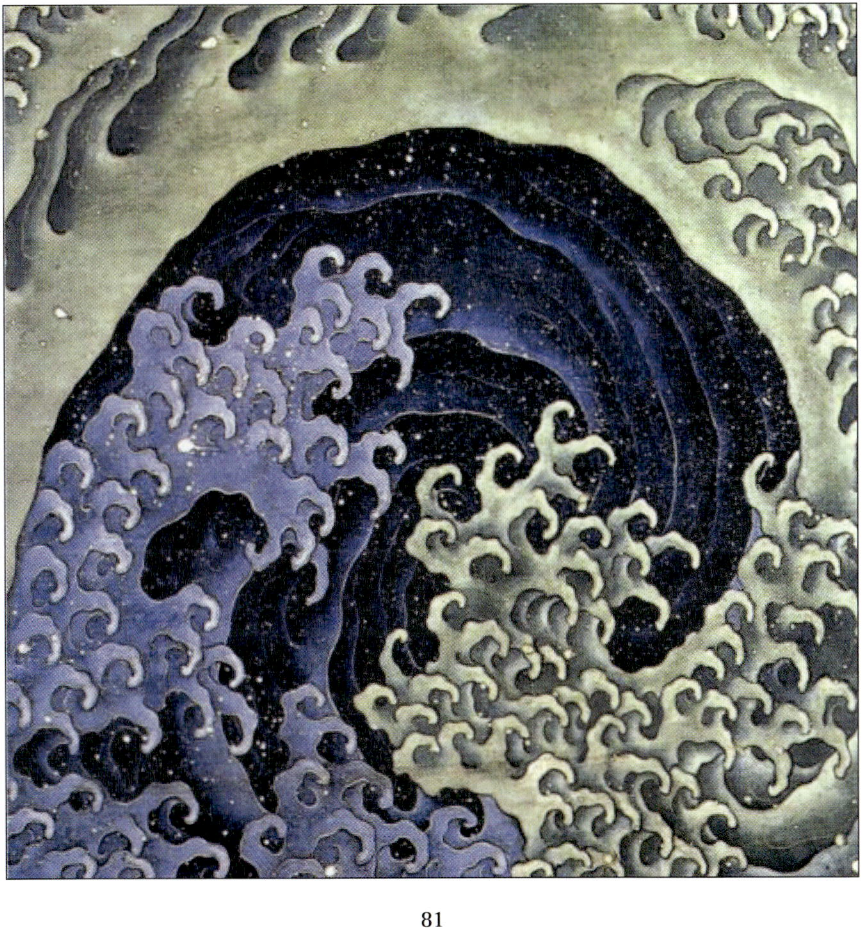

Plate 68

THE POETESS ONO NO KOMACHI

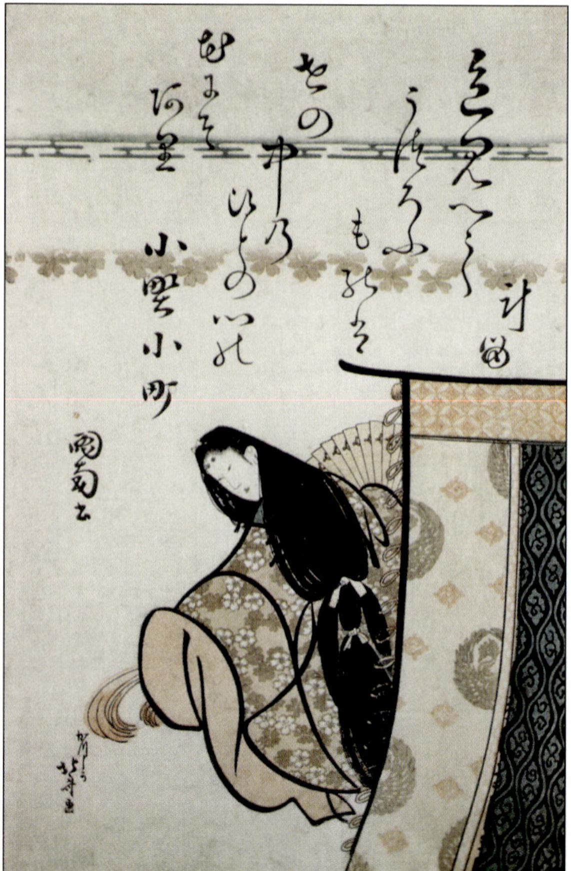

A HAND PUPPET

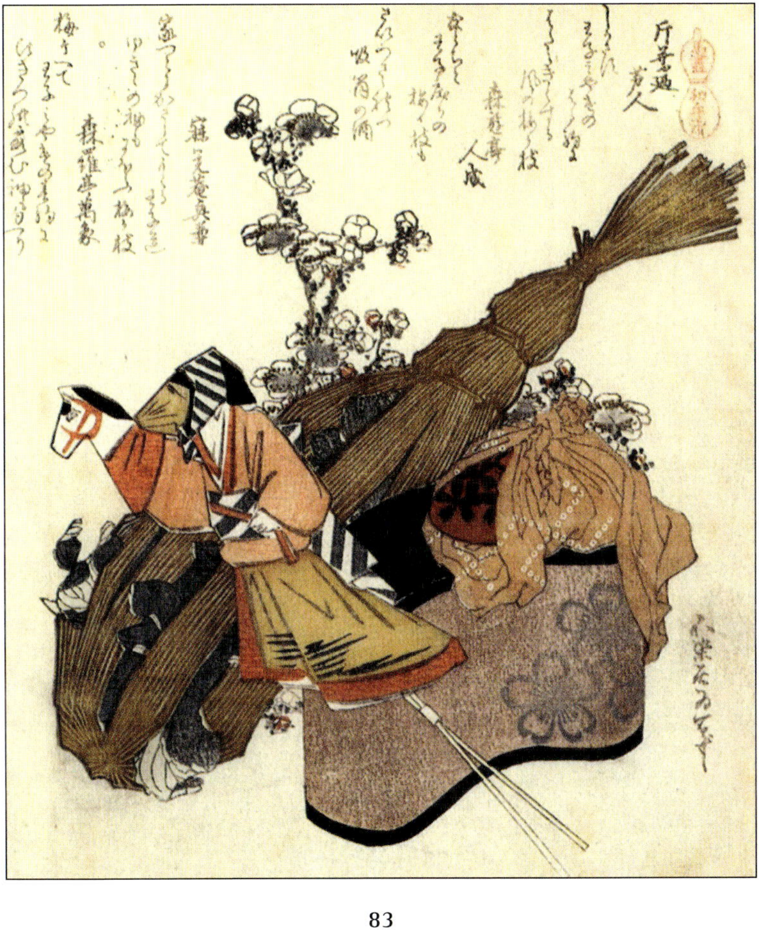

Plate 70

FISHING AT URAGA IN SAGAMI PROVINCE

c. 1834, from Oceans of Wisdom

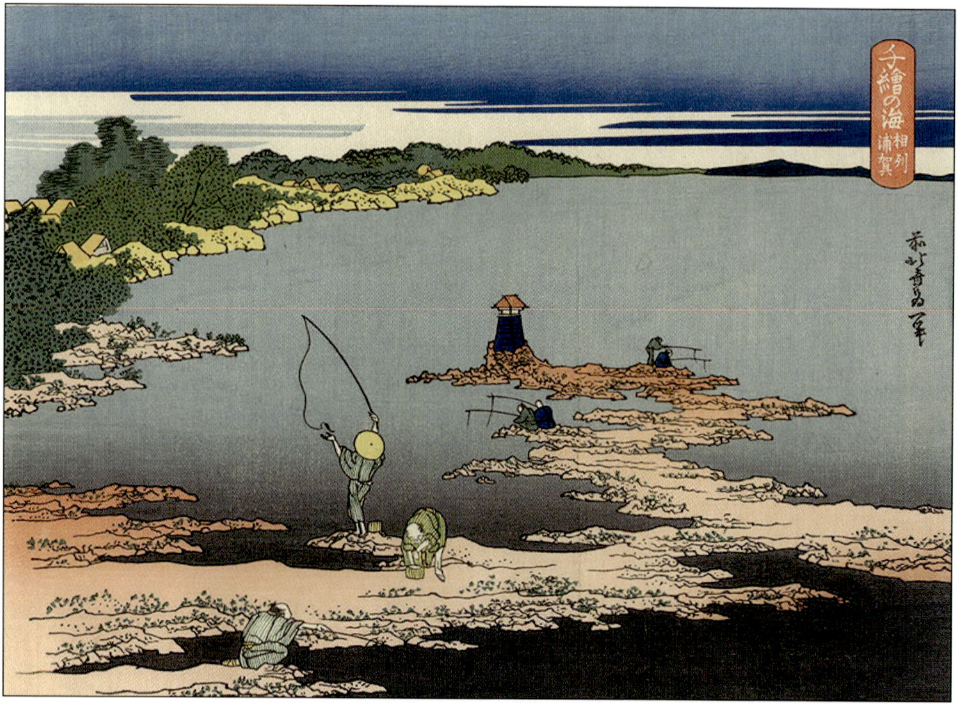

Plate 71

WHALING AT GOTO

c. 1834, from Oceans of Wisdom

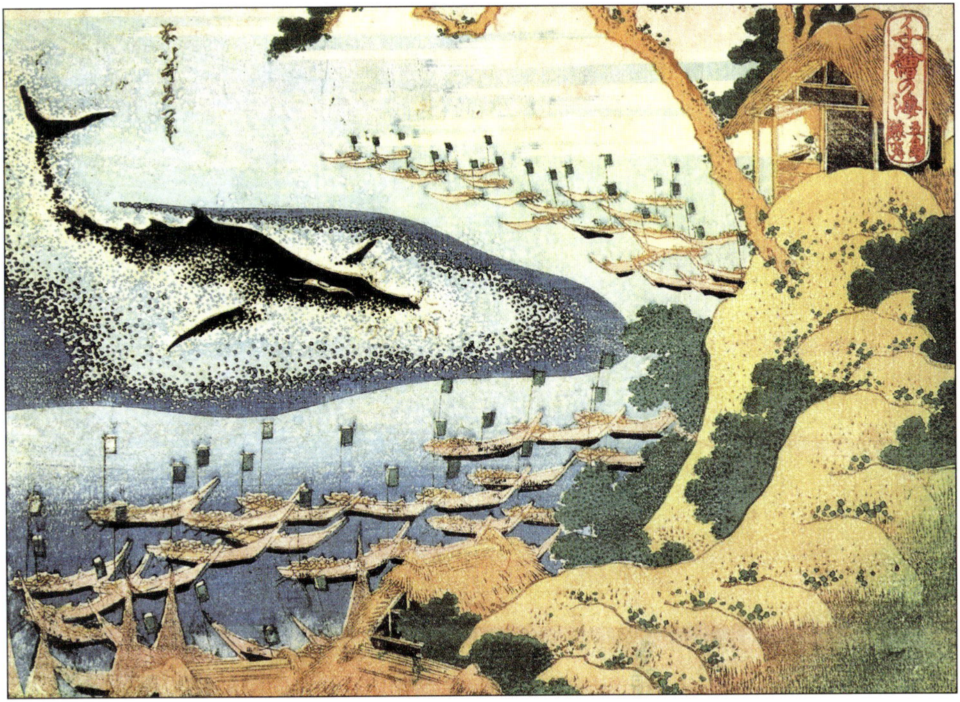

Plate 72

CHOSHI IN THE SHIMOSA PROVINCE

c. 1834, from Oceans of Wisdom

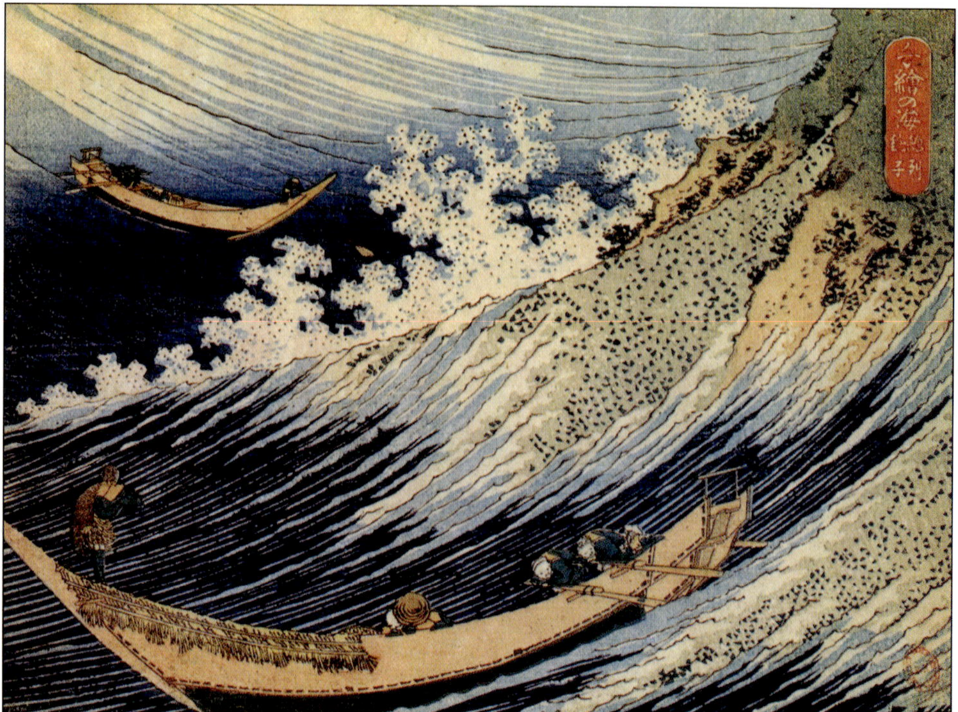

FISHING BY TORCHLIGHT IN KAI PROVINCE

c. 1834, from Oceans of Wisdom

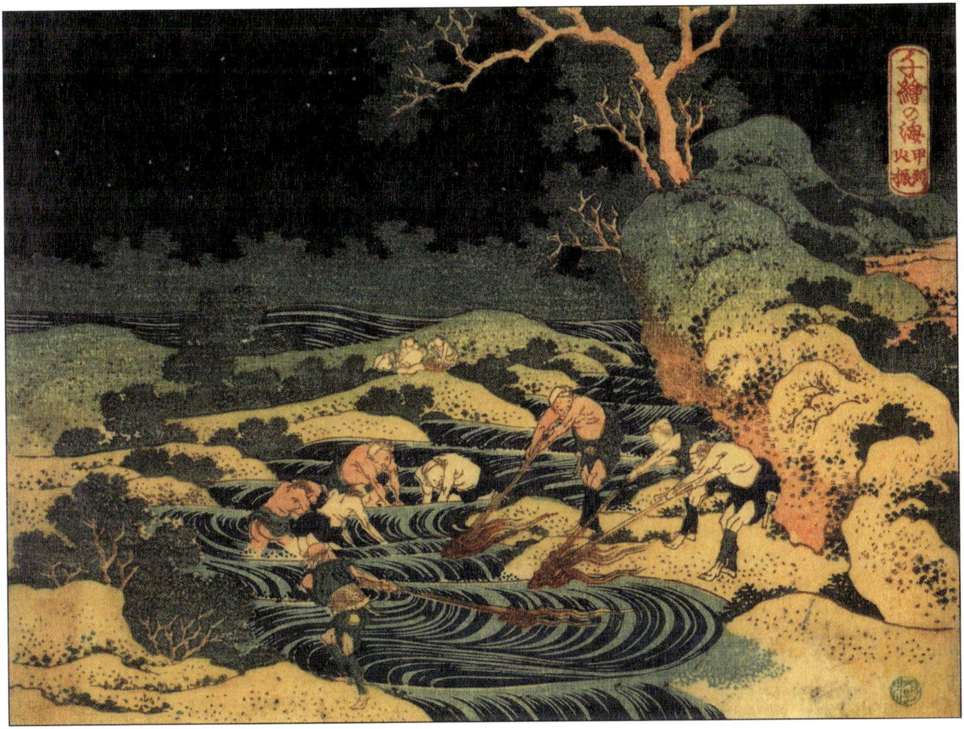

Plate 74

A COLORED VERSION OF THE BIG WAVE

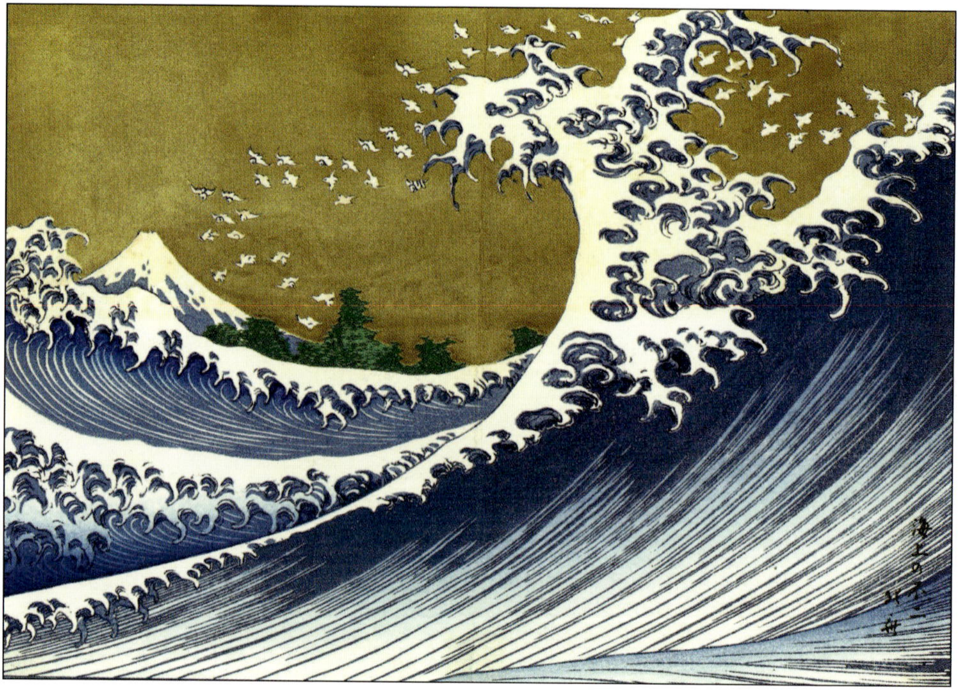

POEM BY ABE NO NAKAMARO

c. 1835–36, from The One Hundred Poems Explained by the Nurse

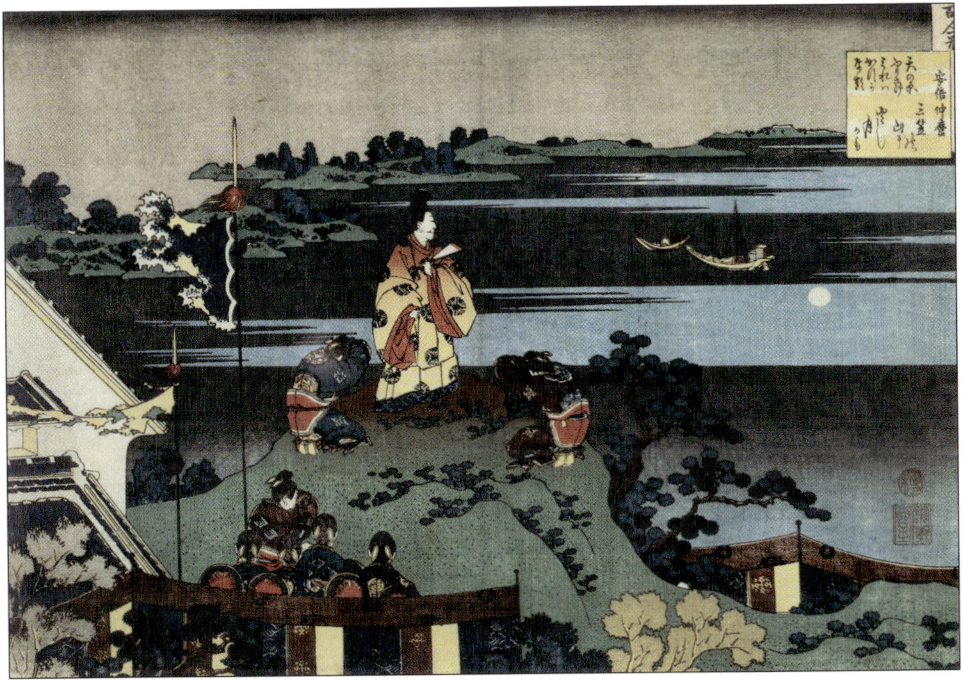

TRAVELERS ON A BRIDGE

c. 1835–36, from The One Hundred Poems Explained by the Nurse

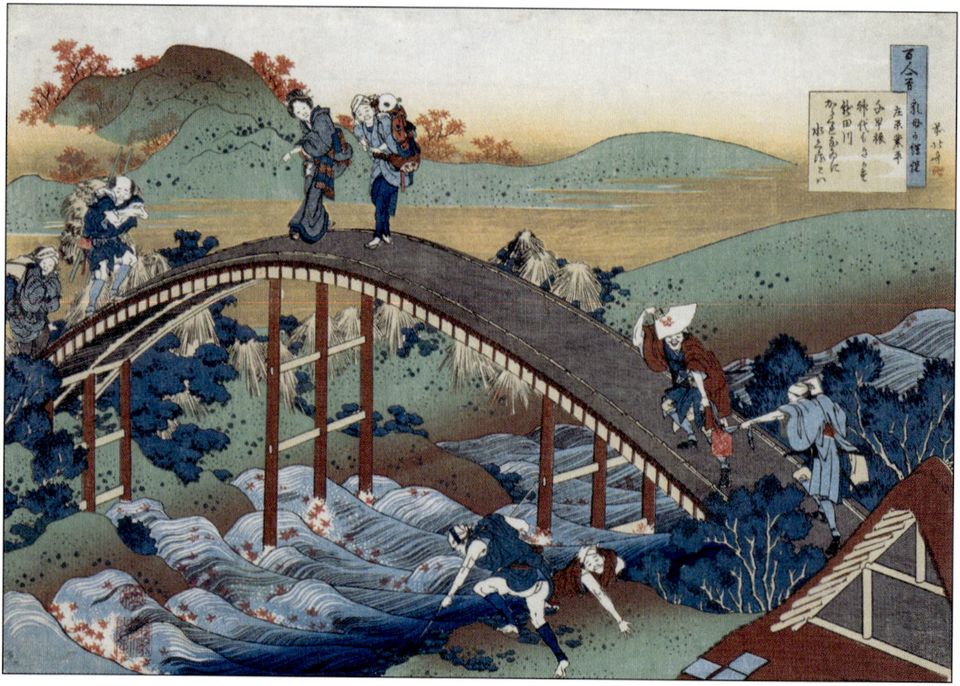

Plate 77

POEM BY KIYOWARA NO FUKAYABU

c. 1835–36, from The One Hundred Poems Explained by the Nurse
Museum of Fine Arts, Boston

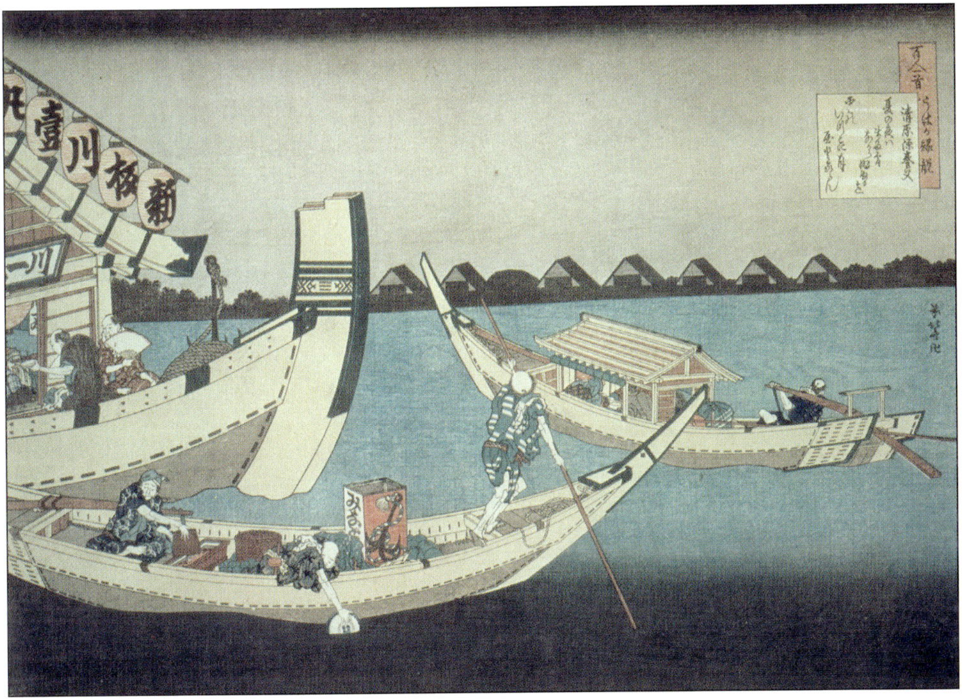

Plate 78

PINK AND RED PEONIES, BLOWN TO THE LEFT IN A BREEZE, AND A BUTTERFLY

c. 1830-31

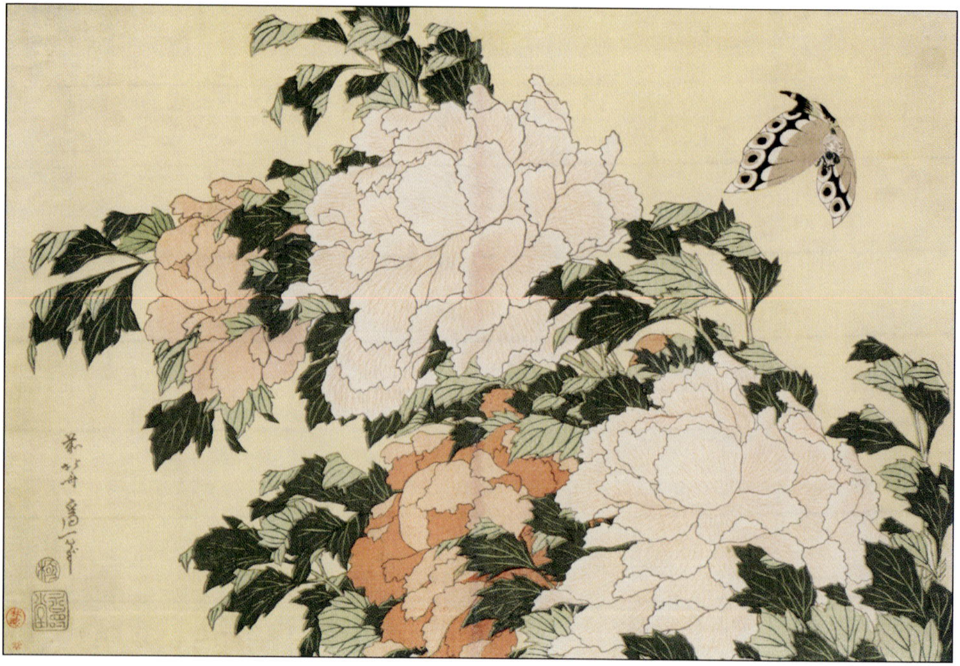

KAKUBAN SURIMONO: FISHERMAN SEATED ON A ROCK

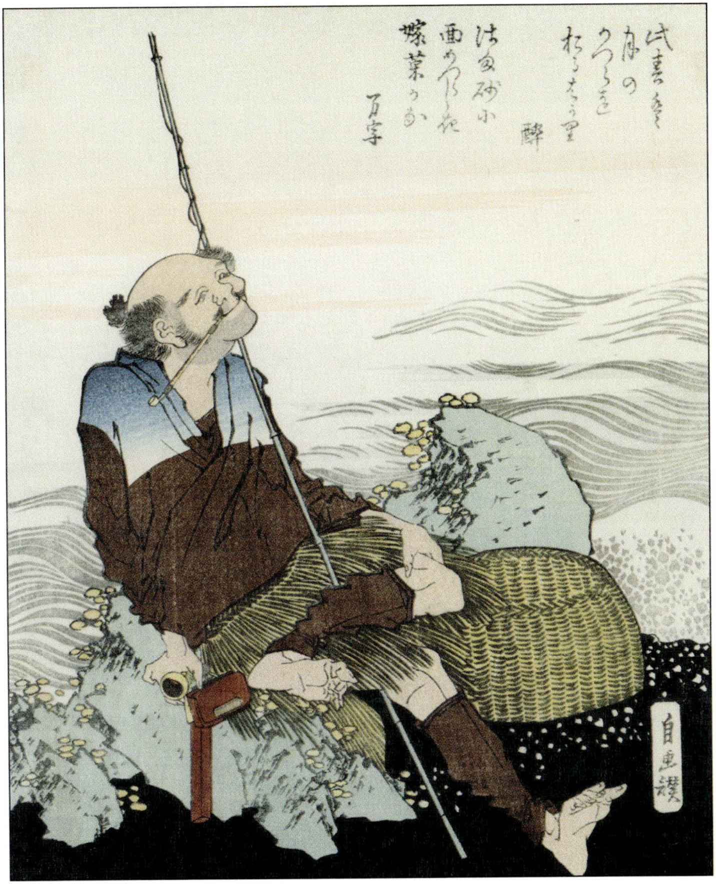

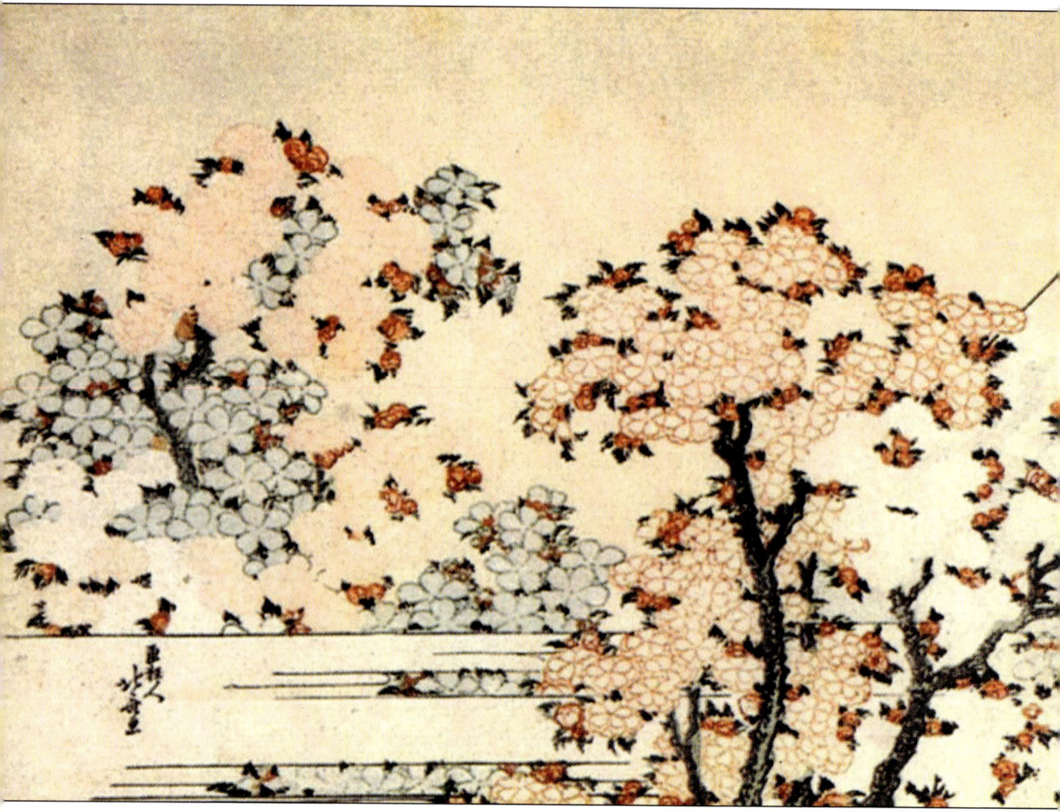

MOUNT FUJI SEEN THROUGH CHERRY BLOSSOMS

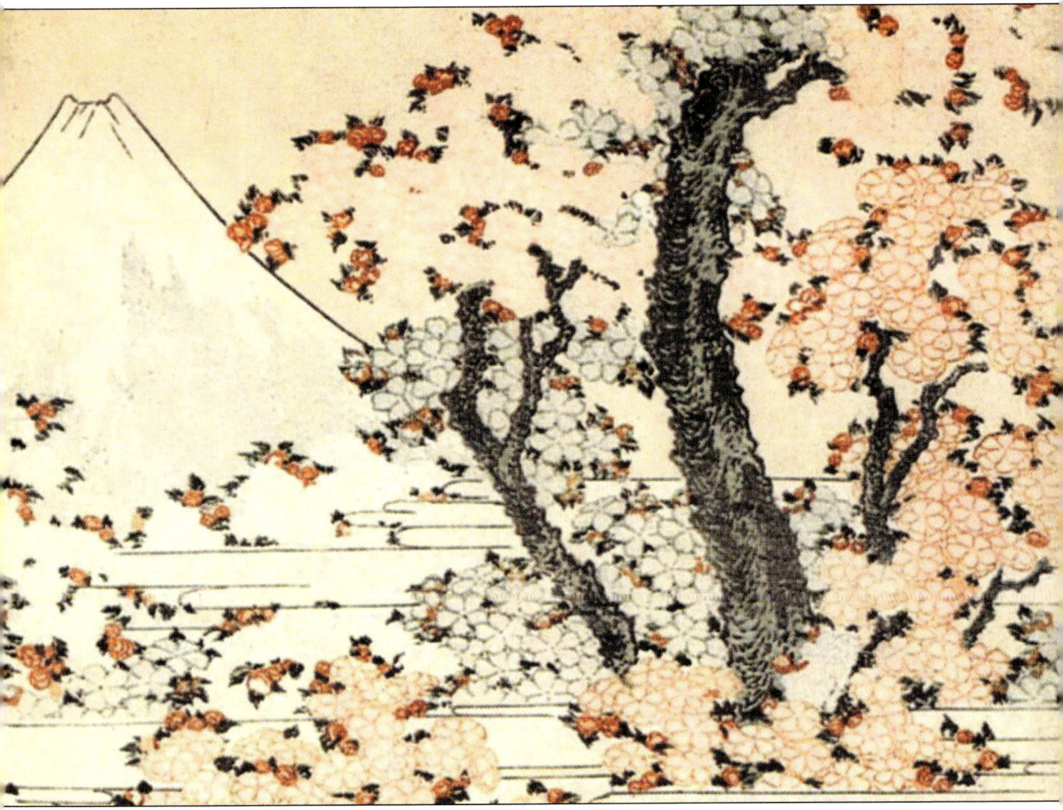

INDEX